ADVISORY COMMISSION

ON

TAXATION AND FINANCE.

FINAL REPORT

OCTOBER, 1908.

NEW YORK:
MARTIN B. BROWN COMPANY, PRINTERS AND STATIONERS,
NOS. 49 TO 57 PARK PLACE.

1908.

MARTIN B. BROWN
PRESS
49-57
PARK
PLACE
NEW YORK

TABLE OF CONTENTS.

Chairman,

EDGAR J. LEVEY.

Committee on Taxation and Revenue.

LAWSON PURDY,
EDWIN R. A. SELIGMAN,
FRANCIS LYNDE STETSON,
JOSEPH HAAG,
EDWARD L. HEYDECKER,
DAVID E. AUSTEN.

Committee on The City Debt and Special Assessments.

EDWARD M. SHEPARD,
JOHN L. CADWALADER
HERMAN A. METZ.
FRANCIS KEY PENDLETON,
FRANK J. GOODNOW.

Committee on Accounting and Statistics.

FREDERICK A. CLEVELAND,
HERMAN RIDDER,
JULIAN D. FAIRCHILD,
JOHN CRANE.
JOHN C. HERTLE.

NEW YORK, October 29, 1908.

Hon. GEORGE B. MCCLELLAN,

Mayor,

The City of New York.

SIR—In February, 1905, you requested the following named gentlemen to serve as an Advisory Commission on Taxation and Finance:

Edgar J. Levey,
John L. Cadwalader,
Morris K. Jesup,
Edwin R. A. Seligman,
Edward M. Shepard,
Charles T. Barney,
Herman Ridder,
Francis Lynde Stetson,
Julian D. Fairchild,
Lawson Purdy,
Frederick A. Cleveland,
John Crane,
John J. Delany,
Frank A. O'Donnel,
Alonzo Bell,
Frank J. Goodnow,
John C. Hertle.

Upon the death of Mr. O'Donnel you appointed Mr. Joseph Haag to fill the vacancy, and in like manner to fill the vacancy caused by the death of Mr. Bell, Mr. Edward L. Heydecker. When Mr. Delany resigned you designated Mr. Francis Key Pendleton as a member of the Commission in his stead. The vacancies caused by the death of Mr. Barney and Mr. Jesup have been filled by Messrs. Herman A. Metz and David E. Austen.

The Commission met on March 6, 1905, and elected Mr. Lawson Purdy as secretary; in your letter you had named Mr. Edgar J. Levey as chairman. Three sub-committees were appointed on

Taxation and Revenue,
City Debt and Special Assessments, and
Accounting and Statistics,

and to them were referred the several subjects mentioned in your letter of appointment. From time to time, as each sub-committee completed its examination of the portion of the work referred to it, it reported to the Commission, and five separate reports have been presented to you by the Commission, copies of which are annexed to this report as appendices.

The first report presented by the Commission was in December, 1905, upon the subject of the City's uncollectible arrears of taxes. It was shown that the uncollected taxes on October 1, 1905, for the years 1898 and prior, amounted to $12,700,872.39, and that the uncollected taxes outstanding on October 1, 1905, for the years 1899 and 1904 inclusive, amounted to $50,823,942.21, making a total of $63,524,814.60.

The Commission has made an estimate of the exact sum uncollectible and had found it to amount to $33,791,172.95, of which amount over $30,000,000 was on account of uncollected personal taxes. The method by which this conclusion was reached and the reasons supporting it are fully set forth in the report submitted to you on December 22, 1905. Having ascertained the total of uncollectible taxes, also having ascertained that this sum was increasing under the methods in force at the time by a sum approximating $3,000,000 a year, the Commission undertook the drafting of legislation to meet this condition, and submitted a series of bills to the Legislature of 1906. Three of these bills were enacted as chapters 207, 208 and 209 of the Laws of 1906.

By chapter 208 of the Laws of 1906, the Board of Estimate and Apportionment of The City of New York was directed to authorize corporate stock of The City of New York to be issued to any amount equal to so much of the deficiency on the first day of January, 1905, in the product of taxes theretofore levied and deemed by the Board to be uncollectible as shall not have been provided for in prior tax levies or by the issue of corporate stock of The City of New York. The intent of this act is to permit the funding of the total of arrears of uncollectible taxes up to the date named, January 1, 1905, and thereby to wipe out the uncollectible arrears up to that date. When all of the corporate stock authorized by this act shall have been issued the uncollectible arrears up to January 1, 1905, will have been funded and will disappear from the City's books of accounts as unpaid taxes.

By chapter 209 of the Laws of 1906, amending section 248 of the Greater New York Charter, the Board of Estimate and Apportionment was directed annually to include in the budget a sum equal to so much of the deficiency on the preceding first day of January in the product of taxes theretofore levied and deemed by the Board to be uncollectible as shall not have been provided for in prior tax levies or by the issue of corporate stock of The City of New York or by such corporate stock, duly authorized by said Board to be issued. The intent of this law is to provide a way by which the amount of uncollectible taxes, ascertained each year, may be included in the budget for the ensuing year and may be stricken off from the City's books of accounts as assets. Under the operation of these two laws, when the discretion vested by them in the Board of Estimate and Apportionment shall have been fully exercised, no uncollectible arrears should any longer appear on the City's books of accounts as assets.

The other law enacted in 1906, printed as chapter 207, adding section 894-a to the Greater New York Charter, was intended simply to cure an administrative defect. By its provisions the Department of Taxes and Assessments was authorized on giving ten days' personal notice to the party in interest, to add to the assessment-rolls of the current year such valuations of real and personal estate as may have been omitted from such assessment-rolls on the first day of the opening of such books. This power did not exist prior to the passage of this law.

The second report of the Commission was presented in December, 1906, and was a review of the question of the taxation of personal property. The report considered the effect of the taxation of personal property in The City of New York, and found that the law was impracticable of operation and unfair in so far as it was enforced. The Commission did not present any drafts of bills to carry out its conclusions, but recommended that this question is of immediate importance to the City, and suggested for your consideration the desirability of bringing the matter to the attention of the Governor and the State Legislature.

This report was quoted with approval by the Charter Revision Commission of 1907, and they recommended that the question of personal property taxation should be submitted to a vote of the people of The City of New York.

In December, 1907, a report was presented by the Commission on the collection of arrears of real estate taxes and assessments. This report reviewed the existing method of enforcing the payment of arrears of real estate taxes and assessments and water rents, and found that these methods were wholly inadequate to enforce the rights of the City. Accordingly, the Commission reported a bill to amend the Greater New York Charter relative to sales of lands for taxes, assessments and water rents, which was enacted by the Legislature of 1908, and which went into effect on October 1, 1908.

By the provisions of this Act the old method of enforcing such charges by the sale of a lease was abolished and in its place is substituted a method requiring the sale of the tax lien of the City to the person who will pay into the City Treasury the amount of the taxes, assessments and water rents, with interest, penalties, and charges, for the lowest rate of interest upon a competitive bidding. The lien of the City is to be transferred to the purchaser by an instrument to be known as a "transfer of tax lien," and which by the terms of the Act is assimilated as closely as possible to a mortgage on real estate. The delinquent taxpayer is allowed three years in which to pay off and discharge this transfer of tax lien, and in the event of his default the foreclosure of the tax lien is provided for in a court of record by a procedure similar to the foreclosure of a mortgage. The substance of this change is the substitution of a judicial foreclosure whereby the rights of all parties in interest may be protected for the administrative act of the Collector of Assessments and Arrears in an ex parte proceeding. As the law became operative on October 1, 1908, the Commission is unable to report upon the results of its administration, but it believes that the Collector of Assessments and Arrears will be successful in collecting the greater part of the arrears of real estate taxes, assessments and water rents, by means of the active and efficient efforts which he is taking to carry out the provisions of the Act.

In April, 1907, the Commission submitted a report on the City debt in its relation to the constitutional limit of indebtedness, containing a proposed amendment to section 10 of Article VIII. of the State Constitution. This report carefully considered the question of the margin of debt incurring capacity of the City. It was ascertained that on January 1, 1907, this margin amounted to $31,143,218.73, and that the total bonded indebtedness of the City at that time amounted to the sum of $544,522,362.23. The report also considered the factors enlarging the City's future debt incurring capacity, and also the probable future indebtedness to be incurred, and reached the conclusion that if it is inevitable that the debt incurring power of the City should be enlarged such enlargement should be accomplished only by authorizing the exclusion from the bonded indebtedness to be charged against the City's debt limit, of bonds issued for the acquisition of property or for the construction of railroads, docks or other improvements, owned by the City, from which the City receives current net income in excess of the interest payable by the City, and that any constitutional amendment designed to accomplish this should provide a nearly automatic scheme by which, should such enterprises ever become non-supporting, the bonds issued to defray the cost should immediately be counted in estimating the City's indebtedness. In the amendment to section 10 of Article VIII. of the Constitution presented by the Commission in this report, careful provision was made safeguarding the City from the continued exclusion of debt incurred for the acquisition of property not sufficiently productive as to pay interest charges.

This question of enlarging the debt-incurring power of the City was considered by the Legislature of 1908, and an amendment to section 10 of Article VIII. of the Constitution, based upon the report of the Commission, was passed by the Legislature.

In June, 1907, the Commission presented a report on the system of accounts and statistics of The City of New York. The existing system was analyzed and its defects pointed out. Briefly, these were shown to be (1) a lack of a system of controlling accounts; (2) a lack of uniformity of an accounting system in the different departments, and (3) a lack of control over expenses incurred in the different departments, and (4) a failure to furnish detailed information as to expenses incurred. The Commission suggested the outline of a general accounting system whereby in addition to securing uniformity of accounting, the Comptroller should be given a wider control over the departmental accounting heads. The Commission also suggested that the Comptroller's office is overburdened with administrative detail, and presented alternative recommendations designed to remedy this condition.

The Commission has considered the propriety of a change in the time for collection of taxes, and has reported its conclusions against the proposed change. The real reason for the urgent demands made during the past few years for a change in the date for the collection of taxes is the large deficiency in the collection of taxes. The past deficiencies due to uncollectible taxes have been provided for by the authorization of an issue of corporate stock and current deficiencies are provided for annually in the budget under the provisions of the laws enacted pursuant to the reports of this Commission. A further deficiency in the current funds of the City is due to the inability of the City to enforce the collection of taxes on real estate. The former remedy for the collection of taxes on real estate by the sale of leases was so ineffective that it has been resorted to but six times in thirty-two years. The amendment to the charter reported by this Commission and enacted by the last Legislature will relieve this situation, and under these changes the Commission believes that the reasons for the suggested change will disappear.

We have reported upon all the subjects submitted for our consideration, and bills have been enacted to carry out our recommendation for legislation.

In May, 1905, $12,000 was appropriated for the expenses of the Commission, and the sum of $3,456 has been expended, mainly for printing. There will be no further expenses except the printing of this report.

Having completed the work assigned to us, we respectfully present this as our final report and request our discharge.

EDGAR J. LEVEY, Chairman.
LAWSON PURDY, Secretary.

LETTER OF THE MAYOR TO CHAIRMAN OF THE COMMISSION.

City of New York.
Office of The Mayor.

November 5, 1908.

Edgar J. Levey, Esq.,
Chairman Advisory Commission on Taxes and Finance,
No. 135 Broadway, N. Y. City:

My Dear Sir—I have received the final report of your Commission, and desire to express to you and, through you, to the members of the Commission, my heartiest thanks for the service you have rendered to the City since your appointment in February, 1905.

The problems the Commission was requested to consider were difficult of solution and of vital importance to the City. You have labored earnestly and with remarkable efficiency.

The Legislature was so impressed by the character of the Commission and with the clear and logical presentation of the reasons for its recommendations, that the laws were enacted as proposed without agitation and without opposition. The Commission has brought to the consideration of these problems the highest order of ability in law, finance and administration. It would hardly have been possible for the City to have secured for hire the services rendered without compensation by you and your associates.

Respectfully,

(Signed) Geo. B. McClellan,
Mayor.

ADVISORY COMMISSION

ON

TAXATION AND FINANCE.

REPORT

OF

COMMITTEE ON TAXATION AND REVENUE

ON

UNCOLLECTIBLE ARREARS OF TAXES, ETC.

DECEMBER, 1905.

LETTER OF TRANSMITTAL.

NEW YORK, December 22, 1905.

Hon. GEORGE B. MCCLELLAN,
Mayor of The City of New York:

DEAR SIR—Among the subjects which your Advisory Commission on Finance was requested to consider is that of the City's uncollectible arrears of taxes. This subject was mentioned in your last annual message to the Board of Aldermen and was specifically referred to this Commission by your letter of February 28, 1905, in the following manner:

"Methods of collecting and enforcing the payment of taxes in The City of New York, bearing in mind the ever-increasing amount of uncollected personal taxes and the difficulty of properly conducting the finances of the City with the product of the tax levied each year falling further and further behind the total appropriation."

Your Commission regards this question not only as one of the most important referred to it for consideration, but also as one which calls for immediate and comprehensive reform. Having reached certain practical conclusions in regard thereto, which have been embodied in drafts for bills to be prepared for legislative action, your Commission desires at this time to make a partial report, so that action thereon need not await the further deliberation required for the other subjects now engaging your Commission's attention.

At a meeting of your Commission, held December 20, 1905, the Committee on Taxation and Revenue presented a report and the Commission unanimously adopted the following resolution:

Resolved, That the partial report of the Committee on Taxation and Revenue be and hereby is accepted and adopted as a report of this Commission, and that it be transmitted to the Mayor as a partial report of this Commission upon the matters submitted for its consideration, with a suitable explanatory letter from the Chairman and Secretary.

In accordance with this resolution, we present to you herewith the partial report of the Committee on Taxation and Revenue. This report is the result of very careful consideration upon the part of the committee, which has had frequent meetings since its appointment in March.

In the report will be found a statement showing the uncollected taxes for the years 1898 and prior at October 1, 1905, and a statement of uncollected taxes for the years 1899 to October 1, 1905, in which is shown the actual levy, the amount collected, discounts, cancellations, uncollected balances, and the amount provided in tax levies for deficiency in the product of taxes. We have analysed these tables and explained the reason why under the provisions of the Charter and Tax Law of the State a very large amount of taxes is in arrears, of which more than one-half is uncollectible. We have made an estimate of the exact sum uncollectible and it amounts to $33,791,172.95. Of this amount over $30,000,000 is on account of uncollected personal taxes. About one-third of the tax levy on personal property each year is uncollectible. This will continue to be the case so long as we have our antiquated system of imposing taxes on all forms of personal property in the same manner as upon real estate. In practice, through what may be no fault of the Department, many persons are assessed for personal property who have no property and from whom in consequence no tax can be collected.

By skillful methods of financing the City, which we approve, it has been possible up to the present time to carry on the City's affairs without increasing the City debt on account of the large deficiency, except as it has been necessary to issue a somewhat larger amount in revenue bonds than should be issued. The limit, however, has been practically reached, and unless provision is made for the existing arrears and for preventing the accumulation of arrears in the future the financial department of the City will be seriously embarrassed.

We were confronted with two problems. First, to provide for the existing arrears, and second, to provide for an annual clearance of future arrears.

To provide for existing arrears we propose an act directing the Board of Estimate and Apportionment to authorize corporate stock of The City of New York to be issued to an amount equal to so much of the deficiency on the first day of January, 1905, in the product of taxes theretofore levied and deemed by the Board to be uncollectible, as shall not have been provided for in prior tax levies or by the issue of Corporate Stock of The City of New York. At first sight this may appear to increase the City's debt, and hence to limit the amount which may be borrowed for needed public improvements. A closer study shows, however, that in order to provide the necessary funds for current expenses the City is now issuing revenue bonds for the account of taxes of previous years which are still uncollected, and these revenue bonds form part of the City's debt which limits its borrowing capacity. The proposed act does not require the immediate issue of the Corporate Stock authorized by the Board of Estimate, but it may be issued in such amounts, from time to time, as may be deemed wise by the Comptroller, to retire outstanding revenue bonds issued in anticipation of the collection of taxes of previous years, and to provide funds to meet payments upon the contract libilities of the City when the money provided for such payment by previous issues of Corporate Stock has already been used for the current expenses of the City. We are satisfied that the City must be empowered to borrow an amount equal to the uncollectible deficiency in the taxes of past years, and it is cheaper for the City to borrow this money on Corporate Stock than on revenue bonds as it is doing to-day.

For reasons which we explained in our report the provisions of chapter 639 of the Laws of 1905 authorizing continually recurring issues of Corporate Stock to make good these deficiencies, we consider objectionable and not in harmony with the plan we propose. We have therefore recommended its repeal.

The second problem, consisting of the annual deficiency in the product of taxes, we have met by providing that the Board of Estimate and Apportionment shall annually insert in the budget a sum equal to so much of the deficiency on the preceding first day of January in the product of taxes theretofore levied and deemed by the Board to be uncollectible, as shall not have been provided for in prior tax levies or by the issue of Corporate Stock of The City of New York, or by such Corporate Stock authorized by said Board to be issued. This is accomplished by an amendment to section 230 of the Charter which shall take effect October 1, 1906. By this act we propose to repeal the section of the Charter which authorizes and directs the Board of Aldermen to increase the tax levy to make good a deficiency in the product of taxes, a provision of law which is quite inadequate and requires an estimate of future conditions instead of a dealing with past and known quantities. But as that section will not be repealed until October 1st the Board of Aldermen in August, 1906, will increase the tax levy for 1906 by the usual amount added for the deficiency. At the meeting of the Board of Estimate in October they will insert in the budget for the tax levy of 1907 an amount which will provide for all uncollectible arrears not theretofore provided for up to January, 1906. Thereafter every year the Board of Estimate and Apportionment will provide for all deficiencies in the collection of taxes so far as the same are uncollectible up to the first of January preceding.

In our report we have explained exactly how we arrive at the amount of the uncollectible arrears, and the method of financing the City by which it has been enabled to pay its bills in spite of the large arrears. We have explained how it may be determined that taxes are uncollectible, and the method of computing the City debt.

Report as to the Propriety of a Change in the Time of Collecting Taxes.

Another subject submitted to the committee for consideration is the propriety of a change in the time for collecting taxes. The committee presents a report made by Mr. Bell upon a proposal to change the date, but the committee concluded that it was not necessary to express an opinion upon the merits of the particular bill discussed by Mr. Bell for the reason that after careful consideration of the whole subject the committee was convinced that it is not desirable to change the present method of providing current funds for the City's needs.

Other Amendments Proposed.

The committee presents two amendments to the charter, and one to the Tax Law, which relate to details of assessment and taxation, and which are sufficiently explained in the report.

Yours respectfully,

Edgar J. Levey, Chairman.
Lawson Purdy, Secretary.

STATEMENT

Showing Uncollected Tax for the Years 1898 and Prior, at October 1, 1905.

Arrears of Taxes, 1898 *and prior:*

Personal—Manhattan and Bronx	$9,323,475 99	
Brooklyn	741,057 49	
		$10,064,533 48

Arrears of Taxes, 1898 *and prior:*

Real Estate—Manhattan	$1,321,608 73	
Bronx	233,204 89	
Brooklyn	303,154 90	
Queens	528,370 39	
Richmond	250,000 00	
		2,636,338 91
Grand total		$12,700,872 39

STATEMENT OF UNCOLLECTED TAXES.

October 1, 1905.

	Levy.	Collections.	Discount.	Cancellation.	Balance Uncollected.	Amount provided in Tax Levies for Deficiency in Product of Taxes.
Tax of 1899: R. E.	$72,805,832 37	$71,202,347 89	$371,375 65	$225,411 09	$1,006,697 74	
Franchises	....	....	....	....	....	
Personal	13,374,238 71	8,483,454 31	53,061 95	436,370 01	4,401,352 44	
	$86,180,071 08	$79,685,802 20	$424,437 60	$661,781 10	$5,408,050 18	$1,689,877 81
Tax of 1900: R. E.	$66,788,643 92	$64,617,688 02	$369,340 02	$818,671 78	$982,944 10	
Franchises	4,969,748 58	2,629,446 40	....	577,482 26	1,762,819 92	
Personal	10,780,850 04	7,595,187 48	55,938 18	438,953 16	2,690,771 22	
	$82,539,242 54	$74,842,321 90	$425,278 20	$1,835,107 20	$5,436,535 24	1,618,473 98
Tax of 1901: R. E.	$70,706,974 60	$68,518,370 53	$366,780 88	$603,101 90	$1,218,721 29	
Franchises	4,925,291 84	1,479,770 43	....	455,070 70	2,990,450 66	
Personal	12,609,537 31	7,026,472 46	42,519 93	828,755 83	4,711,789 09	
	$88,241,803 75	$77,024,613 47	$409,300 81	$1,886,928 43	$8,920,961 04	1,726,169 24
Tax of 1902: R. E.	$71,254,215 12	$69,036,816 14	$388,875 36	$309,577 84	$1,518,945 78	
Franchises	5,049,106 47	1,067,156 66	....	455,842 09	3,526,107 72	
Personal	11,925,231 48	6,357,956 74	40,053 18	913,080 22	4,614,141 34	
	$88,228,553 07	$76,461,929 54	$428,928 54	$1,678,500 15	$9,659,194 84	1,730,018 42
Tax of 1903: R. E.	$64,567,381 13	$62,042,327 06	$365,974 96	$114,028 28	$2,045,050 83	
Franchises	3,360,543 42	499,355 33	....	2,862 71	2,858,325 38	
Personal	9,703,863 56	4,888,803 75	32,553 28	612,962 45	4,169,544 08	
	$77,631,788 11	$67,430,486 14	$398,528 24	$729,853 44	$9,072,920 29	1,522,209 07
Tax of 1904: R. E.	$72,715,090 97	$67,598,533 24	$445,608 14	$119,707 02	$4,551,242 57	
Franchises	3,837,072 69	599,745 25	....	6,363 92	3,230,963 52	
Personal	9,516,239 76	4,802,018 24	35,587 65	134,559 34	4,544,074 53	
	$86,068,403 42	$73,000,296 73	$481,195 79	$260,630 28	$12,326,280 62	1,687,667 20
Aggregate	$508,889,861 97	$448,445,449 98	$2,567,669 18	$7,052,800 60	$50,823,942 21	$9,974,415 72

Recommendations Concerning the Deficiency Caused by Arrears of Uncollectible Taxes.

PROPOSED BILLS.

Draft of an Act to Authorize the Board of Estimate and Apportionment in The City of New York to Issue Corporate Stock of the City for Arrears of Uncollectible Taxes.

Section 1. The board of estimate and apportionment of The City of New York shall on or before the first day of October, 1906, authorize corporate stock of The City of New York to be issued to an amount equal to so much of the deficiency, on the first day of January, 1905, in the product of taxes theretofore levied and deemed by the board to be uncollectible, as shall not have been provided for in prior tax levies or by the issue of corporate stock of The City of New York. Such corporate stock shall be authorized to be issued by the board of estimate and apportionment without the concurrence or approval of any other board or public body.

Section 2. This act shall take effect immediately.

Draft of an Act to Amend the Greater New York Charter by Providing for the Levying of Taxes to Provide for Deficiencies in the Actual Product of Taxes Theretofore Levied.

Section 1. Section 230 of the Greater New York Charter is hereby amended by inserting a new subdivision to be subdivision first; subdivisions first to ninth to be numbered second to tenth, respectively, and the new subdivision to read as follows:

First—A sum equal to so much of the deficiency, on the preceding first day of January, in the product of taxes theretofore levied and deemed by the board to be uncollectible, as shall not have been provided for in prior tax levies or by the issue of corporate stock of The City of New York, or by such corporate stock duly authorized by said board to be issued.

Section 2. Section 248 of the Greater New York Charter is hereby repealed.

Section 3. By this section repeal chapter 639 of the Laws of 1905, amending section 169 of the charter.

Section 4. This act shall take effect October first, 1906.

Memorandum as to Arrears of Taxes and Proposed Amendment.

On October 1, 1905, the uncollected taxes of The City of New York for preceding years amounted to the total sum of $63,524,-814.60. Of this amount, $35,196,206.18 are taxes on personal property, $13,959,941.22 are taxes on real estate other than special franchises, and $14,368,667.20 are taxes on special franchises.

This is an enormous sum, and increases at the rate of more than three million dollars a year. The condition is not due to any fault of city officials, but is wholly the result of unwise and inadequate charter provisions. In order that the remedy which we propose may be thoroughly understood it is necessary first to explain somewhat fully the law and practice governing the financial management of the city, and show how and why there should be so large an amount of taxes uncollected.

The charter requires that the estimate of city expenses for the following year shall be made in the month of October. When this estimate is complete and approved by the Board of Estimate and Apportionment it is called the Budget. It cannot be increased but may be diminished by the Board of Aldermen. When approved by the Board it must be raised by taxation. The taxable property of the city is assessed in the autumn months, the books are opened in January, closed at the end of March, and delivered to the Board of Aldermen the first week in July. The Comptroller certifies to the Board of Aldermen the amount of the Budget and the estimated revenue from the general fund. It is thereupon the duty of the Board to add an amount not exceeding 3 per cent. of the sum to be raised by taxation to provide for deficiencies in the actual product of taxes levied. The Board then determines the rate of taxation which will be necessary to raise the amount of the Budget, including the deficiency item, less the revenue from the general fund. The assessment rolls with the warrants for the collection of taxes are now sent to the receiver of taxes, and taxes become due and payable on the first Monday of October.

The practice of the Board of Aldermen for many years has been to provide a smaller sum for the deficiency than the 3 per cent. allowed; whereas in fact the deficiency has been considerably more than 3 per cent. The deficiency in the collection of taxes comes about in the following ways:

A discount is allowed for the payment of taxes before the first of November, and this decreases the actual collection.

There are some cases every year in which assessments of real estate and personal property are reduced by an order of the court after procedings brought to review the action of the Tax Commissioners. When the court reduces the assessed valuation of real estate or personal property the amount of tax lost to the City swells the deficiency.

These two items, however, are small compared with the very great discrepancy between the amount of the tax actually levied upon personal property and the amount collected. This will continue to be the case so long as we have our antiquated system of imposing taxes on all forms of personal property in the same manner as upon real estate. In practice, through what may be no fault of the department, many persons are assessed for personal property who have no property, and from whom in consequence no tax can be collected. The amount of the tax on personal property which cannot be collected has run as high as one-third of the total amount levied. For five of the six years since consolidation the amount of the uncollected taxes on personal property has only once been less than four million dollars, and in two years was more than four and a half millions.

The Amount of the Deficiency.

In an appendix to this report we present tables showing the actual levy of taxes on real and personal property and special franchises, the amount of the collections, discounts, cancellations, uncollected balances, and the amount actually provided in the various tax levies for deficiencies in the product of taxes.

From these tables it appears that the arrears of taxes for the years prior to 1899 amount to $12,700,872.39. Of this amount $2,636,338.91 is the tax upon real estate, and most of it is collectible. A very small part of it may not be collectible because of the peculiar conditions existing in some of the outlying boroughs prior to consolidation. The arrears of personal taxes levied prior to 1899 amount to $10,064,533.48, and probably no part of this can ever be collected.

From 1899 to the first of October, 1905, the total arrears of taxes due and uncollected is $50,823,942.21. This amount is the uncollected balance after deducting the total discounts and the total cancellations. The discounts have amounted to $2,567,-669.18, and the cancellations have amounted to $7,052,800.60, making a total sum lost to the City through discounts and cancellations of $9,620,469.78. The amount provided in the tax levies of the years 1899 to 1904 for deficiencies in the product of taxes amounts to $9,974,415.72. This sum exceeds the actual loss through discounts and cancellations by the sum of $353,945.94. This is the entire provision for the uncollectible portion of the balance of uncollected arrears of over fifty million dollars.

The amount of the uncollected arrears from 1899 is apportioned as follows:

Personal taxes	$25,131,672 70
Real estate	11,323,602 31
Special franchise taxes	14,368,667 20
Total	$50,823,942 21

The taxes on real estate amounting to over eleven million dollars are practically all collectible, together with interest at the rate of 7 per cent. from the time the taxes became due. Of the tax on special franchises amounting to over fourteen millions there will be a considerable loss on account of the taxes for the years 1900 to 1902. This is occasioned by the fact that the Special Franchise Tax Law requires the State Board of Tax Commissioners to assess special franchises at their full value while other real estate was not assessed as the law directs. When proceedings were brought before Judge Earle to set aside the assessments as unconstitutional, the State Tax Commissioners testified that they had assessed special franchises at full value, and evidence was introduced to the effect that the real estate in The City of New York was assessed at about two-thirds of full value. Judge Earle in his opinion said that "these assessments will have to be reduced at least so much as will equalize them with the other assessments in the same localities."

Method of Financing the City.

For over thirty years the plan of providing the City Treasury with current funds has been through short time loans on what are called revenue bonds issued in anticipation of the collection of the taxes for the current year. It is not contemplated that the City will have any current funds on hand on the first of January, as the taxes of the preceding year will have been used to retire the bonds sold to provide funds for that year. When taxes are paid in October these bonds are retired, and by the first of January the City is obliged to borrow. The charter provides that revenue bonds shall be issued in anticipation of the collection of taxes, and these revenue bonds do not form part of the City debt until they are outstanding for over five years. The debt is limited in amount to 10 per cent. of the assessed value of real estate.

In view of this general plan one would naturally expect that there would be now outstanding revenue bonds to the total amount of the uncollected arrears of taxes, and that these bonds would be divided according to their date of issue in accordance with the amount of taxes uncollected for each of the years for which there are arrears outstanding. If we disregard the arrears of taxes levied prior to consolidation and the finances of the City had been managed as one would suppose from reading the charter, we should have had the following condition on October first, 1905:

Total uncollected taxes for the years 1899 to 1904, inclusive		$50,823,942 21
Less the unapplied balances of the amounts included in the tax levies for deficiencies	$353,945 94	
Less also unexpended balances of appropriations for the years 1899 to 1904, inclusive	6,523,746 79	
		6,877,692 73
Balance		$43,946,249 48

Revenue bonds issued in anticipation of the taxes for the years 1899 to 1904 should be outstanding to the amount of this balance.

The actual condition, however, is far different. The outstanding revenue bonds which were issued in anticipation of the taxes for these years are actually as follows:

Revenue bonds of 1902	$2,700,000
" " 1903	2,100,000
" " 1904	5,200,000
Total	$10,000,000

—a difference of $33,946,249.48. The question now arises, where did the City get this large sum of money by the use of which it has avoided the issuance of revenue bonds, and why has this course been followed?

The funded debt of The City of New York is incurred by the issue of what is called the corporate stock of The City of New York. When corporate stock is authorized to be issued for the purpose of providing funds to pay for some public improvement, as a bridge, park or the like, and contracts are duly entered into by the City for the performance of the work or proceedings are instituted for the acquisition of land, the City incurs what is called a contract liability or land liability which immediately counts as part of the City debt. No such contract liability can be incurred until the issue of corporate stock is authorized. In the books of the City we have then on one side the amount of the authorized issue of corporate stock, and on the other side the amount of the contract or land liability. When part of that corporate stock is sold and a corresponding payment is made on account of the liability, that part of the City's debt is altered from a contract or land liability to an actual indebtedness evidenced by the corporate stock issued.

At all times there are a great many contracts in course of performance for which payment is to be made by an issue of corporate stock. It is obviously impossible for the City to issue corporate stock for the amount of each separate contract liability, at the time when payment must be made, to the amount necessary to make the payment. In practice, therefore, in order to obtain the best terms at the sale of corporate stock a large amount of corporate stock is sold at one time for the account of a number of different contracts. For example, a sale may be made of thirty millions of corporate stock. If the City kept this money on hand for the account of the different purposes for which the issue was made until payments are made for those accounts, the City would have great sums on hand for which it could obtain only 2 per cent. from City depositories, while it is paying 3 per cent. or more for the use of the money, and at the same time is obliged to borrow for current needs on revenue bonds at a rate of interest varying from 2½ to 5 per cent.

Instead of carrying this large sum in City depositories to the credit of the different accounts for which the corporate stock was issued, the money when received is deposited to the credit of a general fund of the City, in which is also deposited the proceeds of such revenue bonds as may be sold and the money received from current tax levies, assessments, excise taxes, etc. The City then having put its money from all these sources into one general fund it uses this fund to retire revenue bonds and to pay current expenses as well as to make the necessary payments on account of the contract liabilities as they become due.

By this practice, instead of having $43,000,000 in revenue bonds outstanding upon which interest must be paid at a rate averaging over 3½ per cent., and having a bank balance in excess of the actual balance in the banks of over $33,000,000, upon which the City would only obtain 2 per cent. interest, the City has had a small balance in the bank and has borrowed at a lower rate on its corporate stock than it could have borrowed upon short time revenue bonds.

To express this practice in simple language it may be said that the City borrows from its own funds provided for special contract purposes in order to meet its current expenses. While this practice has been successfully pursued to the present time and has been productive of a large saving to the City, it can only continue to be pursued so long as the funds derived from the proceeds of the sale of corporate stock and the other funds are not actually required for their respective purposes. It has been shown that the debt of the City is annually increasing at the rate of three millions of dollars a year because of the failure to collect the total amount of taxes levied. The City is not paying its way year by year, but is borrowing from the future for current expenses. In the process it has accumulated a very considerable indebtedness on account of uncollectible taxes.

Having explained the conditions that exist we are now confronted with the problem of existing arrears of uncollectible taxes and of the annual deficiency which will continue to increase unless provision is made for the future.

Existing Deficiency Caused by Arrears of Uncollectible Taxes.

We have already shown the total amount of the arrears of taxes, a part of which is uncollectible. The amount which is uncollectible is too large to raise by taxation in any one year, and in order to make good the deficiency, provision must be made for the issuance of corporate stock to the amount of the existing arrears which are uncollectible. The records of the receiver of taxes and of the Law Department contain sufficient data to determine with almost absolute accuracy the exact amount of the arrears that are uncollectible; but even without a thorough inspection of the records of these departments an estimate may be made which will be sufficiently accurate for the purposes of this report. It may be said with certainty that practically all the arrears of personal taxes levied prior to 1899 are uncollectible, and that all personal taxes levied from 1899 to 1903 which are in arrears are uncollectible. The loss on account of special franchise taxes for the years 1900 to 1902 will not exceed one-third of the levy, and from this must be deducted the amount already canceled which is offset by deficiency items. The total amount is reduced by the balance of the amount provided for deficiencies. The amount of uncollectible arears is therefore about as follows:

Uncollected personal taxes levied prior to 1899..		$10,064,533 48
Uncollected personal taxes levied from 1899 to 1903		20,587,598 17
One-third of the special franchise taxes of 1900, 1901 and 1902.	$4,981,382 29	
Less amount of cancellation......	1,488,395 05	
		3,492,987 24
		$34,145,118 89
Less balance of amount provided for deficiencies in prior tax levies......................		353,945 94
Total		$33,791,172 95

The Committee therefore proposes the passage of an act which shall require the Board of Estimate and Apportionment to authorize the issue of corporate stock of The City of New York to an amount equal to so much of the deficiency on the first day of January, 1905, in the product of taxes theretofore levied and deemed by the Board to be uncollectible, as shall not have been provided for in prior tax levies or by the authorization of the issue of corporate stock of The City of New York.

It is to be noted that the Committee does not propose to require the immediate issue of the corporate stock authorized. It will not be necessary to issue all that is authorized until the needs of the city shall demand it. The issue may be distributed over several years if sufficient funds are on hand to meet payments as they fall due.

On the average The City of New York spends every month more than eight million dollars for ordinary purposes, and four or five millions on account of permanent improvements, so that even should the Comptroller find it expedient to issue at one time the whole amount of bonds authorized, the proceeds would pay the city bills for only two or three months. In view of the existing deficit in the funds provided for permanent improvements the money at the command of the Comptroller will not be excessive.

THE ANNUAL DEFICIENCY.

The existing law to provide against an accumulation of arrears is inadequate, as has already been shown; it is contained in section 248 of the Charter, by which the Board of Aldermen is directed to include in any ordinance imposing and levying taxes such sum as the Board shall deem necessary, not to exceed three per centum, to provide for deficiencies in the actual product of the amount of taxes imposed and levied. The arrears exceed three per cent., so that this power is insufficient; moreover, it is made the duty of the Board to make an estimate as to the future. It is far better to deal with known quantities than with future estimates, and by the amendment we propose all arrears will be provided for annually in the Budget.

By chapter 639 of the Laws of 1905 an attempt was made to provide for the deficiency in the collection of personal taxes, by amending section 169 of the Charter. The amendment provides that corporate stock of The City of New York shall be issued to the amount of personal taxes in arrears for five years. This provision is inadequate in that it does not provide for the deficiency caused by the uncollectible taxes on real estate. The amendment is undesirable because it provides for a continuous increase in the indebtedness of the City, by the amount of uncollected personal taxes; it, moreover, fixes a standard of uncertain character. Instead of providing for taxes which are uncollectible, it provides for all which are five years in arrears, which may or may not be uncollectible. It is proposed, therefore, to repeal the amendment to section 169 of the Charter, adopted in 1905.

Section 230 sets forth the mandatory items to be included in the annual estimate. It is proposed to amend this section by requiring the Board of Estimate to include in its final estimate a sum equal to so much of the deficiency, on the preceding 1st day of January, in the product of taxes theretofore levied and deemed by the Board to be uncollectible, as shall not have been provided for in prior tax levies or by the authorization of the issue of corporate stock of The City of New York.

By the passage of the act providing for the issue of corporate stock to supply the uncollectible deficiency in the product of taxes outstanding January 1, 1905, all arrears on that date will be funded. The proposed amendment to section 230 adheres to the same language, so that there will be an annual clearance of all uncollectible arrears, and an erroneous estimate of one year will be corrected the following year.

In October, 1906, the Board of Estimate will include in the Budget all uncollectible arrears as the same shall be on January 1, 1906, and annually thereafter the amount of all uncollectible taxes outstanding on the first of the year must be provided for in the Budget.

Section 248, being superseded, will be repealed after the deficiency item is added to the tax levy for 1906.

WHAT TAXES ARE UNCOLLECTIBLE.

The question has been considered whether it is desirable to define just what taxes are uncollectible, or to leave this determination to the Board of Estimate, and the conclusion has been reached that it is best to leave this administrative detail to the Board without definite instructions. The Comptroller is a member of the Board, and the Receiver of Taxes is a subordinate of the Comptroller. The Receiver of Taxes has records which furnish most of the information necessary. The additional information required can be obtained from the Corporation Counsel, who is required to advise the Board of Estimate or any officer of the City.

Taxes on Real Estate.

Taxes on real estate are uncollectible when assessments are reduced, or in the case of exempt property vacated, by judicial decision, or by the action of the tax commissioners. When such decisions are rendered an order is served upon the receiver of taxes and his records show the amount of the tax lost.

Taxes on Personal Property.

There is a large amount of taxes on personal property which is uncollectible. The fact that such taxes are uncollectible can in most cases be ascertained with certainty. The facts appear in the following ways:

First—All taxes on personal property for the collection of which no action has been commenced within the time limited by section 934 are outlawed and uncollectible. When the attorney for the collection of arrears is satisfied by sufficient evidence that the person assessed has no property liable to execution, actions are not pressed. The records of the Bureau for the Collection of Arrears of Personal Taxes show such cases.

Second—All cases in which the assessment has been reduced or vacated by judicial decision. This may happen in four ways: When the assessment has been vacated or reduced as a result of a review of the action of the Tax Commissioners upon a writ of certiorari; when the assessment has been vacated because the person assessed was a non-resident; when pursuant to an offer of judgment a part of the tax has been accepted as payment in full; when pursuant to section 934 of the Charter or section 259a of the Tax Law an order has been entered remitting part or all of the tax.

Third—All cases in which the tax has been remitted or reduced by the tax commissioners after the delivery of the tax rolls to the receiver of taxes.

Fourth—Taxes for the collection of which actions have been brought, judgments obtained, executions issued and returned unsatisfied. These cases offer about the only element of uncertainty, for a judgment is good for twenty years, and although worthless at present, it may sometime have a value. At the same time a chance of anything ever being collected on such judgments is very remote.

It will be observed that all the facts necessary to determine whether taxes on personal property are collectible or not are within the knowledge of the Corporation Counsel and Receiver of Taxes.

Method of Computing the City Debt

In order that the financial methods of the City may be better understood in connection with this report we present the following summary of the manner of computing the debt of the City for the purpose of determining its borrowing capacity or margin for incurring further indebtedness. The borrowing capacity is arrived at as follows:

From the 10 per cent. of the assessed valuation of real estate for purposes of taxation there is deducted:

1st. The net funded debt.

2nd. The liability incurred by the City on account of contracts entered into, in excess of the credit balances in the funds or accounts, applicable to such contracts.

3rd. The liability incurred by the City for lands acquired in excess of the credit balances in the funds applicable thereto.

4th. The liability of the City for judgments against the corporation.

5th. Revenue bonds issued in any year for account of taxes levied in prior years.

Net Funded Debt.

The gross funded debt includes all stocks and bonds except revenue bonds issued in anticipation of taxes. The net funded debt is arrived at by subtracting from the gross funded debt the amount of the various county debts and also the amount of the gross funded debt held by the Commissioners of the Sinking Fund for investment for account of the various sinking funds.

Contract Liability.

The liability on contracts is arrived at by deducting from the estimated cost of the several contracts, the payments made on account and the balance to the credit of the fund or account provided for the liquidation of each contract liability. The balance then remaining is treated as indebtedness on account of contracts.

Land Liability.

The liability for lands acquired includes all property, the title to which has vested in the City, but which has not been paid for.

The cost is estimated where actual figures are not obtainable and the estimate is usually based upon tax valuations furnished at the time when the proceeding to acquire the property is authorized by the Board of Estimate and Apportionment. From such estimated cost, or actual cost where it is known, there are deducted the balances standing to the credit of the accounts or funds ultimately chargeable with the obligation. If a fund or account is chargeable with contract liability, as well as land liability, the balance to the credit of the fund is first applied on account of the contract liability and the surplus, if any, applied in reduction of the land liability. The balances thus arrived at are treated as liability for lands acquired.

Liability for Judgments.

The estimated amount of $2,000,000 is usually carried as indebtedness on account of judgments, this being considered a very liberal estimate.

Revenue Bonds.

Revenue bonds issued in anticipation of the collection of taxes for years prior to the years of issue are treated as debt. The Constitution provides:

"This section shall not be construed to prevent the issuing of certificates of indebtedness or revenue bonds issued in anticipation of the collection of taxes for amounts actually contained or to be contained in the *taxes for the year when such certificates or revenue bonds are issued* and payable out of such taxes."

Report as to the Propriety of a Change in the Time of Collecting Taxes.

Your Committee presents a report made by Mr. Bell upon the bill introduced in the Legislature of 1905, by which it was sought to advance the date for the payment of taxes in order to obviate the necessity for borrowing money in anticipation of the collection of taxes. It is not necessary for the Committee to express an opinion upon the merits of this particular bill, for the reason that after careful consideration of the whole subject your Committee is convinced that it is not desirable to change the present method of providing current funds for the City's needs. Briefly described, the present plan is this: The City starts the fiscal year on the first of January with practically no money, and receives no income until the first of October, when taxes are payable. During this time the City is authorized to borrow on short time revenue bonds to meet current expenses, these bonds being issued in anticipation of the collection of the taxes for the current year. These bonds are not a charge against the City's debt limit. Under ordinary circumstances the City pays from 2½ to 4 per cent. interest on these short time loans, though in exceptional times of tight money the City has to pay a higher rate.

Those who object to this method of financing the City contend that it is wasteful and costly for the City to live on borrowed money for its current needs, because of the amount of interest that has to be paid, which is a charge upon the taxpayers. It is moreover often assumed that this condition is the result of carelessness and extravagance in past years, and not of any carefully planned system. The fact is, however, that this method was adopted after due consideration for what your Committee believes to be good and sufficient reasons. Under the present method there is not at any time in the City Treasury a sum of money in excess of the balance which the City should have on hand, whereas under any plan which would obviate the necessity for borrowing there would be large sums in the City Treasury far in excess of its necessities. Upon such large sums the City could not obtain a high rate of interest. Ordinarily it receives 2 per cent. upon its deposits in city banks and trust companies. While the City has been fortunate in having men of thorough integrity and great ability at the head of the Finance Department, the Committee does not deem that it is wise to count too confidently upon there never being an exception to that condition, and put upon the Comptroller and Chamberlain the burden of caring for larger sums of money at any one time than is necessary. Indeed, the Comptroller and Chamberlain would have difficulty in properly placing fifty millions of dollars or more which they might have on hand in case the City were relieved of the necessity of borrowing for current needs. It is clear that the burden of caring for so large a sum would be onerous, and the temptation to grant favors by the disposition of deposits would be severe.

The Committee has fairly faced the only argument advanced, which is that if the City were not obliged to borrow, the sum now paid as interest would be saved to taxpayers. This argument appears to be without merit. The only source from which the City can obtain current moneys is the payment of taxes. If taxpayers provide a sum sufficiently large to obviate the necessity for borrowing, the taxpayers lose the use of the money so advanced, which presumably in any state of the money market is worth more to taxpayers than the interest which the City could obtain for deposits in banks and trust companies. Thus under ordinary circumstances the City pays for loans 3 per cent. or 3½ per cent. and obtains 2 per cent. upon its deposits. Under such conditions the money is certainly worth more to the taxpayers, as a rule, than the 3 per cent. or 3½ per cent. which the City is obliged to pay. If, on the other hand, the conditions of the money market are such that the City is obliged to pay the highest rate of interest, under these conditions again the money is worth more to the taxpayers, for such use as they can make of it, than the sum the City has to pay in interest.

These considerations and perhaps others were undoubtedly in the minds of those who devised the system under which The City of New York has been financed for thirty years and more. Without regard to the merit of any particular plan which may be advanced for obviating the necessity of borrowing in anticipation of the collection of taxes, the Committee believes that the present plan is the best which can be devised under all the circumstances as they now exist.

Report of Mr. Bell Upon the Bill to Advance the Date for Payment of Taxes.

G. O. No. 32. SENATE BILL No. 118,329. INT. 103.

AN ACT to Amend the Greater New York Charter, as Amended by Chapter 466 of the Laws of 1901, and Subsequent Amendments Thereto, Relative to Levying Taxes and the Collection Thereof.

OBJECTIONS.

This bill seeks, through amendments to twenty-seven sections of chapter 466 of the Laws of 1901 (Greater New York Charter), to so change the law relating to assessments and taxation that taxes now *due* and *payable* on the first Monday in October of each year *may be paid* on the first Monday in January of the same year, thus advancing the collection of taxes nine months—the object sought by this advancement being to do away with the present necessity of issuing short term bonds in anticipation of the collection of the tax revenue.

If the object could be attained by this bill the estimated saving in interest would be about $1,500,000 each year.

The plan of the bill, however, is so radically defective that it ought not to become a law.

The plan of the bill proceeds upon the theory that the only way to advance the payment of taxes nine months is to arbitrarily do away with the field work, revision, hearings and other details hitherto and under existing law deemed essential to a just and legal assessment.

To secure this arbitrary assessment the duplicate of the 1906 roll is to be " used as the basis for determining the amount of tax to be levied on real and personal estate of the several boroughs for the year 1907 (section 892*a*)."

The books containing these duplicate assessments are to be open for public inspection, examination and correction from the second Monday in January to the first day of April, 1906. On the last-named day the books " shall be closed, to enable the Board of Taxes and Assessments to prepare assessment rolls of the several boroughs for delivery to the Board of Aldermen " (section 892).

During the months of April and May the Commissioners may act upon applications, take testimony, examine applicants for the reduction of assessments, provided such applications were filed prior to the thirty-first day of March preceding (section 895, New York Charter).

Section 2 of the new bill provides:

> "Nothing in this act contained shall be deemed or construed as repealing or amending any of the sections of the Greater New York Charter, as amended by chapter 466 of the Laws of 901, in so far as they in any way relate to the making of the budget, and also the annual record of assessed valuations of the real and personal estate of the several boroughs on which the taxes for the year 1905 and 1906 are to be determined, nor is it to affect in any way the levying or collection of the taxes for said years 1905 and 1906, but the said budget and annual records for said years shall be prepared and the levying and collection of the taxes for said years shall proceed in the manner now provided by law and as if the act had not been passed."

As the act is to take effect on the first day of June, 1905, it is clear that the reservation in section 2, above quoted, applies only to the assessments and taxes for the years 1905 and 1906.

It would appear equally clear that the only specific reservation of the old law affecting the duplicate roll for 1907 is that provided for in the new section 892a, as follows:

> "Both of said records (1906-1907) shall be subject to the provisions contained in section 892 of this act, except that the said records shall remain open for public inspection, examination and correction from the second Monday in January until the first day of April in said year, 1906. The second or duplicate record shall be used as the basis for determining the amount of tax to be levied on real and personal estate of the several boroughs for the year 1907."

Section 2 provides that:

> "The annual record of assessed valuations for the taxes to be levied for the year 1907 shall be subject to the same changes and corrections as the annual record of assessed valuations for the taxes to be levied for the year 1906;

such corrections and changes shall be made within the same period, at the same time and in the same manner on each of said records; provided, however, that if it shall be found necessary, by reason of changes in valuations of real and personal property subsequent to the preparation of said annual record, to make additional changes or corrections, that such additional changes or corrections may be made at any time prior to the first of September, 1906, but no increase in valuations by reason of said changes shall be made, except upon notice given to the individual or corporation affected by such increase, at least ten days before the fifteenth day of August of said year."

From this it may be fairly construed that the duplicate rolls for 1907 are open for public inspection, examination and correction from the second Monday of January until the first day of April, 1906, as provided in amended section 892a of the new bill, and that under section 2 of the act parties assessed thereon may be heard by the Commissioners during April and May upon applications for reduction of assessments upon either real or personal property filed in their offices on or before the thirty-first day of March, 1906.

The proviso in section 2—that changes and corrections may be made in the rolls of 1907 at any time prior to the first day of September, 1906, if "found necessary by reason of changes in valuations of real and personal property subsequent to the preparation of said annual record," can hardly be construed as authorizing the addition of new names or new entries upon the rolls for 1907, after the first day of April, or any hearing whatever, to those assessed on said rolls, except to those whose assessments are to be increased. Taxpayers in this class are entitled to notice, and, consequently, may be heard on such notice at any time prior to September 1, 1906. The vast majority of the property-owners assessed on the 1907 rolls, for no better reason than that they were liable on the rolls for 1906, have no opportunity to be heard under this bill. Their real estate in 1907 may be less in value than in 1906, because of the destruction of the improvements thereon or for other reasons. Their personal property liable in 1906 may have been lost, sold or converted into non-taxable property during that year, yet under this bill they have no opportunity to establish the facts, as no public inspection or examination of the rolls for 1907 after March 31, 1906, is provided for, either through personal notice (except in increase cases) or by publication in the newspapers or the *City Record*, as now required by law.

This deprivation of the right of property-owners to be heard on their assessments before they ripen into a tax is a violation of a fundamental right guaranteed by the State Constitution.

The authorities relied upon to support this conclusion are numerous. Some of the leading ones are included in and commented upon in the case of Stuart *vs*. Palmer, 74 N. Y., 183. In that case the Court says:

> "The Legislature can no more arbitrarily impose an assessment for which property may be taken and sold than it can render a judgment against a person without a hearing. It is a rule founded on the first principles of natural justice, older than written constitutions, that a citizen shall not be deprived of his life, liberty or property without an opportunity to be heard in defense of his rights, and the constitutional provision that no person shall be deprived of these 'without due process of law' has its foundation in this rule. The provision is the most important guaranty of personal rights to be found in the Federal or State Constitution. It is a limitation upon arbitrary power and is a guaranty against arbitrary legislation. No citizen shall arbitrarily be deprived of his life, liberty or property. This the Legislature can not do or authorize to be done. 'Due process of law' is not confined to judicial proceedings, but extends to every case which may deprive a citizen of life, liberty or property, whether the proceedings be judicial, administrative or executive in its nature (Weimer *vs*. Bruienbury, 30 Mich., 201). This great guaranty is always and everywhere present to protect the citizen against arbitrary interference with these sacred rights."

This arbitrary feature of the bill, growing out of the duplicate roll plan, which necessarily creates a tax liability for 1907 during the year 1906, and before the tax for 1906 is due and payable, is so unjust, that no plea of expediency can justify its adoption, and its presence as the basic principle in the McCarren bill should be fatal to its enactment.

The objections to the bill may be summarized as follows:

1. The duplicate roll plan is open to serious objections. No provision is made for the public inspection, examination and correction of the rolls of 1907, except at the time when the books of annual record are open for public inspection, examination and correction of the assessments for 1906. As all property-owners outside of New York have an opportunity to be heard on assessments against them for the year 1907, failure to grant this right in the pending bill is an unjust discrimination against the property-owners of Greater New York.

2. Changing the period for field work from September, October, November and December to January, February, March and April is objectionable. It is transferring important outdoor work from the best to the worst months (except April) in the year. January, February and March are usually cold, wintry months. With snow on the ground it would be difficult to trace boundary lines or identify stakes or monuments, while the low temperature would materially interfere with the work of recording data in the books carried by the deputies. The necessary work could not be properly done in these months.

3. Changing the "grievance" period from the second Monday of January to April 1 in each year—to May 1 to July 1—is unwise. Taken in connection with the period for hearings (April and May), on applications for reductions, filed prior to the closing of the books on April 1, and the change proposed in this bill, confining such work to July and August, we shall have the hottest months of the year for the most important work of the Department, making necessary the presence of the taxpayer and those representing his interests at a time when, usually, they are out of the city for needed recreation and health.

4. By advancing the time for paying taxes on the plan proposed, the loss from the rolls for 1907 would be—loss of the natural increment of values due to growth and improvements for 1906—at least $100,000,000.

Loss from new estates, new residents and newly-organized corporations for the same year, $100,000,000.

Loss of the Special Franchise for 1907, estimated at $375,000,000.

Estimated total loss of assessments to the tax rolls of 1907, $575,000,000, or, at present rates, a loss in taxes of $8,702,165.

5. Amended section 900 of the new bill makes it obligatory on the part of the Comptroller "to prepare and submit to the Board of Aldermen, at least two weeks before its annual meeting in each and every year, for the purpose of imposing the annual taxes, a statement setting forth the amounts by law authorized to be raised by tax." He is required to give "an estimate of the probable amount of receipts into the City Treasury during the fiscal year next succeeded from all the sources of revenue of the general funds, including surplus revenue from the sinking funds of the Mayor, Aldermen and Commonalty of The City of New York, other than the surplus revenues of any such sinking funds for the payment of interest on the City debt of the municipal corporation known as The Mayor, Aldermen and Commonalty of The City of New York, or the like debts of the municipal and public corporations by this act consolidated as aforesaid, and the said Board of Aldermen is hereby authorized and directed to deduct the amount of such estimated receipt from the aggregate amount of all the various sums which, by law, they are required to order and cause to be raised by tax for the purposes aforesaid, and to cause to be raised by tax only the balance of such aggregate amount after making such deductions."

No such obligation is imposed upon the Comptroller in the new bill for the tax year of 1907. As the annual meeting of the Board of Aldermen would be the first Monday of July, 1906, and the report required from the Comptroller under section 900 refers to said annual meeting and tax for 1906, and under the new bill would refer to the annual meeting of the Board of Aldermen October 1, 1907, relating to the tax for 1908, it would appear that no provision has been made in the new bill for this important statement from the Comptroller to the Board of Aldermen at the meeting September 15, 1906, authorized by the new bill, for the purpose of fixing the tax rates on the duplicate assessment rolls for 1907.

6. Section 2 of the new bill required the Board of Taxes and Assessments to certify to the correctness of the rolls of 1907. "The rolls, so certified, must, on the 15th day of September, 1906, be delivered by the Board of Taxes and Assessments to the Board of Aldermen, which shall meet at noon on that day at the City Hall, or usual place of meeting, for the purpose of receiving the same and for the purpose of performing such other duties in relation thereto as are prescribed by law."

As the only duties "prescribed by law" appear to relate to the annual meeting of the Board of Aldermen to be held on the first Monday in July, 1906, for the tax year of 1906, and, under the new-bill, the first day of October, 1907, for the year of 1908, it may be open to question whether the failure in section 2 of the new bill to provide for the Comptroller's statement required under section 900 to be submitted to the Board of Aldermen "at least two weeks before its annual meeting in each and every year for the purpose of imposing the annual taxes," and the further failure to specifically refer to the sections imposing certain duties to be performed by the Board of Aldermen at their annual meeting, or to reiterate the powers therein conferred, do not leave the Board of Aldermen without power to fix the tax rate for the assessments on the duplicate roll for 1907, and to perform other important duties relating to said assessments at their meeting, to be held, as provided in section 2 of the new bill, on the fifteenth day of September, 1906.

7. Section 907 requires the Board of Taxes and Assessments to furnish the Supervisor of the City Record with a copy of the Annual Record of the assessed valuation of real estate within three weeks after the delivery of the assessment rolls to the Board of Aldermen. Under section 1527 (New York Charter) this copy is to be published in the *City Record* within ninety days after the delivery of said copy to the Supervisor. This would require the publication of the assessment rolls of 1906 during the last week of October, 1906, or two weeks after the copy of the duplicate roll for 1907 has been furnished to the Supervisor of the City Record under the same law. As this publication for each year will cost the City from $40,000 to $50,000, it would appear a waste of time and money to publish the assessment rolls for 1907, practically covering the same data as the rolls for 1906 and published within two months after the publication of the rolls for 1906.

8. Under this bill the tax for 1906 becomes "*due and payable*" on the first Monday of October, 1906. The tax for 1907 "may be paid" January 1, 1907, three months after the time when the 1906 tax is due and payable. This will impose a hardship upon the average taxpayer and will force many to borrow money for prompt payment of tax or compel them to defer payment until the tax becomes a lien and interest at 7 per cent. per annum begins to run.

9. Under this bill a rebate of 3 per cent. per annum is allowed on payments made between the 1st of January, 1907, and December 1, 1907. Those who borrow money to pay their taxes must pay 5 or 6 per cent. interest. The rebate allowed is no inducement to those who are forced to borrow or to those who can profitably use their money. Thus, failure to collect the taxes in the early months of the year would defeat the object of the bill and compel the issue of short-term bonds.

10. Beginning the work of assessments at the first of the year instead of the last, makes it impossible to include in the rolls the accretions of the year, due to natural growth, improvements, etc., estimated at $100,000,000; new estates; corporations organized during the year; the personal property of new residents, etc., estimated at $100,000,000. Special franchise assessments estimated at $375,000,000—a total loss in assessments on the rolls for 1907 of $575,000,000, or a tax loss at 1.51 of $8,702,165.

11. Under existing law the tax becomes a lien on the first Monday in October, about 8½ months after the opening of the books of Annual Record for public inspection, etc. Under the new bill the tax becomes a lien October 1 of the year following the preparation of the rolls, or 17 months after the opening of the annual record for public inspection, etc.

12. Under existing law interest on unpaid taxes runs from January 1, or three months and a half after the tax rolls are delivered to the Receiver of Taxes. Under the new bill interest on unpaid taxes runs from October 1 in the year following the delivery of the tax rolls to the Receiver of Taxes, or a period of nine months after the delivery of the rolls to the Receiver.

The accompanying statement shows in comparative form the essential features of the law now in force and the changes therein under the proposed amendments.

SENATE BILL No. 118,329.

Relative to Levying Taxes and the Collection Thereof.

Character of Work.	Under Existing Laws.	Under the Proposed Law.
1. Field Work	1st Tuesday in September to 2d Monday in January	1st Monday in January to May 1.
2. Books open for inspection and correction	2d Monday in January to April 1	1st day of May to July 1.
3. Hearings—on applications filed	April 1 to June 1	July 1 to September 1.
4. Final closing of books and making up roll	June 1 to 1st Monday in July	September 1 to October 1.
5. Certification of rolls to Board of Aldermen	1st Monday in July	1st day of October,
6. Extension of tax on return from Board of Aldermen	From about the 15th of August to the 15th of September	From about the 15th of November to December 1.
7. Copy of rolls to Supervisor of City Record	Three weeks from 1st Monday in July	Three weeks from October 1.
8. Delivery of rolls to Receiver of Taxes.	September 15	December 1.
9. Taxes become *due* and *payable*	1st Monday of October—(15 days after filing with Receiver of Taxes	May be paid 1st Monday of January (30 days after filing with Receiver of Taxes).
10. Taxes become a lien	1st Monday of October—date of filing with Receiver of Taxes	1st Monday of October, or ten months after the rolls have been filed with Receiver of Taxes, or seventeen months after the books are opened for inspection, etc.
11. Time for rebate and rate allowed	October and November—rate 6 per cent. per annum	From January 1 to December 1—rate 3 per cent. per annum.
12. One per cent. penalty	December 1 to January 1	No penalty.
13. Interest begins on arrears—7 per cent.	January 1—(three months after filing with Reciever of Taxes)	December 1 dating from October 1—(nine months after filing with Receiver of Taxes).
14. Taxes may be paid without interest or penalty	From 1st Monday in October to December 1 (two months)	From January 1 to December 1 (eleven months).

Amendment in Relation to Omitted Property.

Under existing law real and personal property not appearing on the assessment rolls on the second Monday of January—the date when the books of annual record are opened for public inspection, examination and correction—cannot be included in the aggregate of assessed valuations subject to taxation.

As the tax liability depends upon the ownership of taxable property on a certain date, it appears unjust that its omission from the rolls on that date, through clerical oversight or otherwise, should place it beyond the power of the taxing authorities, even though its existence may have been brought to their knowledge before the closing of the books. As this is manifestly unjust to the general taxpayer, the Commission recommend the following proposed amendment to the Charter:

AN ACT to amend The Greater New York Charter relative to the power of the Department of Taxes and Assessments to add certain property and names to the assessment rolls.

The People of the State of New York, represented in Senate and Assembly, do enact as follows:

SECTION 1. Chapter four hundred and sixty-six, title one of chapter seventeen, laws of nienteen hundred and one, is hereby amended by inserting therein a new section, to be section eight hundred and ninety-four *a* thereof and to read as follows:

SECTION 894*a*. So long as the books of annual record of the assessed valuation of real and personal estate of the several boroughs remain open for public inspection, examination and correction, the board of taxes and assessments, after giving at least ten days prior personal notice to the party in interest, may add to the rolls of assessment of such annual record any real estate, or the name of the owner of any personal estate, and also the assessed valuation of any such real or personal estate that may have been omitted from such rolls on the day of the opening of such books.

SECTION 2. This act shall take effect immediately.

Amendment in Relation to Applications for Remission or Reduction of Taxes.

The following amendment of section 897, New York Charter, is recommended. Its purpose is to correct the section so as more clearly to express its intent and to place a reasonable limitation on the time within which applications for remission or reduction of taxes may be made to the Board of Taxes and Assessments:

AN ACT to amend The Greater New York Charter relative to the power of the Department of Taxes and Assessments to remit or reduce a tax.

The People of the State of New York, represented in Senate and Assembly, do enact as follows:

SECTION 1. Section eight hundred and ninety-seven of The Greater New York Charter, as amended by chapter one hundred and ninety-two of the laws of nineteen hundred and two, is hereby amended to read as follows:

SECTION 897. At any time within one year after the delivery of the books to the receiver of taxes for the collection of any tax upon real or personal estate if, in the opinion of the corporation counsel lawful cause shall have been shown, the board of taxes and assessments by the vote of a majority of all the commissioners, may remit or may reduce any such tax which by such board shall be found to be erroneous or excessive; but no such tax shall be so remitted or reduced except upon satisfactory proof that application for relief within the period prescribed by other laws for the correction of assessments has been prevented by illness or by absence from the city. Nothing herein contained is intended to affect, or shall affect, any provision of section 934 of The Greater New York Charter or of section 259*a* of the tax law.

SECTION 2. This act shall take effect immediately.

Amendment in Relation to the Refunding by the State of Uncollected Direct Taxes.

AN ACT to amend the Tax Law relating to the cancellation and reduction of assessments and the remission of taxes.

The People of the State of New York, represented in Senate and Assembly, do enact as follows:

SECTION 1. Chapter nine hundred and eight of the laws of eighteen hundred and ninety-six, entitled "An act in relation to taxation, constituting chapter twenty-four of the General Laws," is hereby amended by inserting therein a new section, to be section one hundred and ten thereof, and to read:

SECTION 110. *Assessments Canceled or Reduced.* In every case where an assessment included in the equalized valuation of real and personal property, as fixed by the state board of equalization, shall have been canceled or reduced, or the tax thereon shall have been duly remitted, by final order of the court, or under any provision of law, the state comptroller, on application of the treasurer of the county wherein such assessment shall have been made, or if made in the City of New York, on the application of the comptroller of said city, and on satisfactory proof of such cancellation, reduction or remission, shall cancel, if unpaid, and if paid, shall refund, the state tax imposed and levied upon such canceled or reduced assessment, or included in such remitted tax, provided that within two years after such final cancellation or reduction, or such final remission, application for relief under the provisions of this section shall have been filed with the state comptroller.

SECTION 2. This act shall take effect immediately.

REMARKS.

SECTION 110. The purpose of this amendment is to give authority to the State Comptroller to cancel, if unpaid, and to refund, if paid, any State tax imposed upon assessments that have been legally set aside by final action of the courts, or canceled or reduced by other legal authority, provided such assessments were included in the equalized assessed valuations upon which the State tax was imposed.

The imposition of a tax implies that something exists capable of being taxed. If there is nothing to tax, a tax erroneously imposed should not stand. If the State is convinced that the basis of the tax has been destroyed by the courts or other legal authority, the tax itself should be canceled, if unpaid, or refunded, if paid.

The section gives the City substantially what the City and State give the individual under existing laws—relief from a tax erroneously imposed.

ADVISORY COMMISSION

ON

TAXATION AND FINANCE

COMMITTEE ON

TAXATION AND REVENUE

REPORT

OF

MR. PURDY

ON

THE PERSONAL PROPERTY TAX

JUNE 6, 1905

Report of Lawson Purdy on the Personal Property Tax.

Committee on Taxation and Revenue:

GENTLEMEN—In accordance with your request I submit the following report upon two questions. First: Is it desirable to strengthen the provisions of the law for the collection of taxes upon the personal property of non-residents, and to subject to taxation additional personal property of non-residents? Second: Should the provisions with reference to the deduction of debts from personal assets be so changed that debts may only be deducted from credits?

The literature upon the subject of the general property tax as applied to the taxation of personal property is so voluminous that it seems unnecessary to add to it by any lengthy discussion of the subject as an original contribution. Tax Commissions have been appointed in many of the States to consider questions of this character, and numerous books and pamphlets have been written by students of the subject, which have added greatly to our general knowledge. The brief report which follows is made up almost entirely from quotations from these various treatises and reports. In presenting evidence with regard to the expediency of making any change in the law with reference to the deduction of debts, I have selected those States in which it is not permitted to deduct debts from personal assets other than credits.

The general property tax as applied to the taxation of personal property is so thoroughly discredited that any attempt to make it more effective can only serve to delay its inevitable downfall. The greatest difficulty in securing the repeal of any law imposing a tax is to be found in the amount of revenue which the tax produces. The smaller the revenue the easier it is to repeal the law. It is plain that our law might be changed so as to produce a larger revenue for a time, but in the light of all experience it seems that this would only increase the injustice of the law and render its repeal more difficult.

HISTORY OF THE GENERAL PROPERTY TAX.

* "*Historically,* the property tax was once well-nigh universal. Far from being an original idea which the American instinctively adopted, it is found in all early societies whose economic con-

* The General Property Tax, pp. 60 and 61, Edwin R. A. Seligman, 1890. Also in his *Essays in Taxation.*

ditions were similar to those of the American colonies. It was the first crude attempt to attain a semblance of equity, and it at first roughly responded to the demands of democratic justice. In a community mainly agricultural, the property tax was not unsuited to the social conditions. But as soon as commercial and industrial considerations came to the foreground in national or municipal life, the property tax decayed, became a shadow of its former self and ultimately turned into a tax on real property, while professing to be a tax on all property. The disparity between facts and appearance, between practice and theory, everywhere became so evident and engendered such misery that the property tax was gradually relegated to a subordinate position in the fiscal system and was at last completely abolished. All attempts to stem the current and to prolong the tax by a more stringent administration had no effect but that of injurious reaction on the *morale* of the community. America is to-day the only great nation deaf to the warnings of history. But it is fast nearing the stage when it, too, will have to submit to the inevitable."

Mr. David A. Wells thus sums up the experience of other countries:

* "*Origin and History of the General Property Tax*—The idea that in order to tax equitably it is necessary to assess everything capable of resulting in the obtaining of revenue is not original with the American people. Its inception dates back to the dawn of civilization, and its development may be regarded as in the nature of an economic evolution. In the incipient stages of society, as already pointed out, property consisted exclusively of things tangible and visible—lands, buildings, cattle, slaves, agricultural products, household effects and implements—and what was exacted by rulers or chiefs of their subjects was arbitrary proportions of such kinds of property or of personal service, and was not in any proper sense taxation, but tribute. For thousands of years there were no credits or material evidences of indebtedness, as there are none at the present time among barbarians or half-civilized people; for a knowledge of letters, of the art of writing, and a somewhat durable and portable material to write upon were essential prerequisites for their existence, the earliest evidence of the recognition of anything like a mortgage being the inscription on certain clay tablets excavated from the ruins of

* Theory and Practice of Taxation, pp. 432-437, David A. Wells, 1900.

the ancient cities of Babylon and Assyria, which were evidently the highest results of long and slowly developing civilization. In fact, in the early stages of society there was no important form of capital other than landed property and the instrumentalities, including slaves, for its cultivation, and so far as the system for obtaining revenue for the rulers of state merited the name of taxation, it was practically a 'land' tax.

"As civilization advanced, slavery gradually broke down; trade or traffic between individuals or adjacent communities extended and became commerce; free labor appeared; capital developed and multiplied the forms of visible, tangible property. Then the system of obtaining revenue began to have the characteristics of a general property tax; and as the coincidence of great value with small bulk in some forms of tangible, visible property favored concealment, some methods of obtaining revenue from property other than mere inspection became necessary, and were obtained by the Romans in the latter days of their empire by endowing their assessors and taxgatherers (as before shown) with the power to administer torture to unwilling taxpayers, a method that was followed and perpetuated until within a very recent period by the rulers of most Asiatic countries; and in later days, when credits came into existence and extensive use, and titles to property and evidences of indebtedness were regarded as property, although intangible and invisible, a method of discovering and assessing the same, as approximate to actual torture as a higher civilization would sanction, was everywhere adopted.

* * * * * * *

"After the dissolution of the Roman Empire and the subsequent reconstruction, as it were, of government and society in Europe during the early feudal period, and when land was practically the only form of wealth, the payments exacted for the support of the governing powers—kings, barons, knights, etc.—were essentially and almost exclusively in the nature of land taxes; and the terms '*danegeld,*' a charge on lands at so much per hide, or an area of about one hundred acres; '*scutage,*' a charge on tenants in lieu of military service; '*carucage,*' a charge on 'plough lands'; '*tallage*' (from the French *tailler,* to cut off), a charge on the tenants of royal manors, and the like were designations of the different forms of such assessments at different periods. As civilization advanced and was accompanied, as at a more primitive period, with an increase in the forms of personal property, a combination of taxes on land and movables, or a general property tax system, developed and was adopted by all the nations of western Europe with all the despotic adjuncts which seemed necessary to make its enforcement successful. The ultimate result of such a system was what might have been anticipated. From a very early period it occasioned great popular dissatisfaction. In Milan, Italy, as early as 1208, it was enforced with such severity 'that the assessment book was known as the *libro dei dolore.*' In Florence it became so honeycombed with abuses and the load of taxation fell with such crushing force on the small owners of property that imminent popular revolution and disorder compelled its essential modification. As wealth increased, evasions of the tax increased in a greater proportion in every community, leaving the burden of the system, as now in the United States, on that class of the population—mainly agricultural—that are least able to bear it. Sir Robert Cecil stated in 1592 that there were not five men in London assessed on their goods at two hundred pounds (one thousand dollars); and Sir Walter Raleigh stated in 1601 that 'the poor man' (in England) 'pays as much as the rich.' In Florence in 1495 only fifty-two persons paid the tax on trade capital, although the amount of such capital must have been immense. Marshal Vauban, of France, who wrote on taxation about 1700, stated that the *taille personelle* was assessed only on the poorest classes. The result has been that as the difficulty of assessing visible personal property and the impossibility of reaching invisible and intangible personalty became apparent, the tax was gradually modified, and finally abolished in all European countries, except, possibly, Switzerland and Holland, where its nature has very little of its original and typical character. One of the first acts of the French National Assembly in 1789 was to abolish it entirely. [In England] a provision for taxing personal property under a nominal land tax continued to exist on the statute book until 1833, when, through constant exemptions and systematic evasions, the annual revenue accruing from the same had run down to the sum of eight hundred and twenty-three pounds (four thousand one hundred and fifteen dollars). It is also interesting to note that the people of Europe have been so long exempted from a general property tax that their leading writers on economic or fiscal subjects rarely discuss it or even seem to have any knowledge of its characteristics or historical experience."

"*The Use and Value of Oaths as an Adjunct of Taxation.*—Consideration is properly asked in this connection to the use and value of oaths, an increase in the number and stringency of which is often regarded as essential to effective and equal taxation. It is the all but unanimous opinion of officials who of late have had extensive experience in the administration of both the national and State revenue laws that oaths, as a matter of restraint or as a guarantee of truth in respect to official statements, have in a great measure ceased to be effectual; or, in other words, that perjury, direct or constructive, has become so common as to almost cease to occasion notice. In fact, there has come to be a feeling in the community that an oath in respect to matters in which the Government is a party is a mere matter of form, of mechanical procedure, and that its violation, especially with a mental reservation, and when the interest of other individuals is not specifically affected, does not in itself constitute a crime. The fact that the assessors of almost every State every year make oath that they have valued all property at its actual value, when they know they have not, constitutes one proof of the truth of this assertion. The everyday entry of goods at the custom-house at undervaluation constitutes another; the enormous frauds committed in recent years under the internal revenue laws of the United States, which in the case of distilled spirits entailed a loss in a single year of over $130,000,000, and in which the taking of false oaths was at every step an essential feature, constitutes a third; while of individual examples, which every assessor of experience can detail, the record would be almost interminable.

"During the past few years the low tone of commercial morality in the United States has been a fact generally recognized and much commented upon; but it has not, that we are aware, been made a subject of inquiry by those to whom the guardianship of public morals is particularly intrusted. How far the existing system of laws relating to taxation—national and State—are justly chargeable with the results to which reference has been made, or how much in the division of responsibility is to be set down to the account of those who violate the law, and how much to those who, forewarned of the weakness of human nature, deliberately make laws which especially lead men into temptation, are yet unsettled questions.

"A point of great interest and importance in this connection, though often overlooked, is that even if all the States of the

Federal Union should entirely exempt personal property within their territory and jurisdiction from taxation, it would, nevertheless, owing to the dual nature of the Government of the United States, be subject to a large measure of heavy and disproportionate taxation. Thus, the expenditure of the Federal Government, which represents taxation, was in 1896, including the cost of revenue collection, in excess of $445,000,000, not one cent of which was derived from taxes on real estate. The aggregate of annual taxation by States, counties, cities, municipalities, and the District of Columbia for the same year, is estimated by reputable authorities to have been about $400,000,000, of which at least one-fifth was assessed or was collected from personal property. If real estate paid all the State taxes, personal property, therefore, would still be paying all the United States Government taxes, or a large excess of its equitable share of any or all national taxation. A claim that any personal property owner is justified in protecting himself against such extortion in any and every legal way has much, therefore, to be said in its favor. When such protection cannot be effected legally, he has only to leave the State for others that are not extortionate oppressors of capital. But who cannot perceive on reflection that personal property (capital) must be largely used by its owners and at fair rates at their residence; and that the home of such capital will show the benefit in increased local business, increased population and increased value of real estate by its use? Why, then, so much overrighteous talk of personal property owners dodging taxation?

" Logical and ingenious as have been the arguments in opposition to the legal exemption of personal property from taxation, the citation and consideration of the undisputed experience of all countries, people and ages are all that is necessary to refute and disprove them. There was a time when nearly all men believed and taught that the world was flat, and when the few lisped to the contrary, exposed themselves to a charge of religious heresy and punishment. But a comparatively short navigation experience effectually put an end to all controversy on this subject; and it is doubtless only a question of time when personal property will be exempt from governmental taxation, because no system has ever been devised, or is likely to be, which will enable a State to tax it with any approach to uniformity and equity."

Experience of American States.

OHIO.

It has been claimed by some that the administrative features of the law in certain States are not sufficiently thorough and severe, and for that reason the system has broken down, and not because the system is wrong in itself. This reproach cannot be laid against the law in Ohio. The Constitution of Ohio provides as follows: "Section 2. Laws shall be passed taxing by a uniform rule all moneys, credits, investments in bonds, stocks, joint-stock companies or otherwise; and also all real and personal property according to its true value in money."

The statutes of Ohio require that blanks containing lists of every conceivable kind of personal property shall be sent to every person over twenty-one years of age, who must answer every question relating to the various sorts of property which he owns or are in his keeping, and he must do this under oath and under pain of heavy penalties. In order that the inquisitorial nature of the law may be fully understood, I quote sections 2736 and 2737 of the Ohio statutes:

"Sec. 2736. Each person required to list property shall, annually, upon receiving a blank for that purpose from the assessor, or within ten days thereafter, make out and deliver to the assessor a statement, verified by his oath, of all the personal property, moneys, credits, investments in bonds, stocks, joint-stock companies, annuities or otherwise, in his possession or under his control on the day preceding the second Monday of April of that year, which he is required to list for taxation, either as owner or holder thereof, or as parent, husband, guardian, trustee, executor, administrator, receiver, accounting officer, partner, agent, factor or otherwise."

"Sec. 2737. Such statement shall truly and distinctly set forth, first, the number of horses, and the value thereof; second, the number of neat cattle, and the value thereof; third, the number of mules and asses, and the value thereof; fourth, the number of sheep, and the value thereof; fifth, the number of hogs, and the value thereof; sixth, the number of pleasure carriages (of whatever kind), and the value thereof; seventh, the total value of all articles of personal property, not including in the preceding of succeeding classes; eighth, the number of watches, and the value thereof; ninth, the number of pianofortes, and the value thereof; tenth, the average value of the goods and merchandise which such person is required to list as a merchant; eleventh, the value of the property which such a person is required to list as a banker, broker or stock jobber; twelfth, the average value of the materials and manufactured articles which such person is required to list as a manufacturer; thirteenth, moneys on hand or on deposit subject to order; fourteenth, the amount of credits as hereinbefore defined; fifteenth, the amount of all moneys invested in bonds, stocks, joint-stock companies, annuities or otherwise; sixteenth, the monthly average amount or value, for the time he held or controlled the same, within the preceding year, of all moneys, credits or other effects, within that time, invested in, or converted into, bonds or other securities of the United States, or of his State, not taxed, to the extent he may hold or control such bonds or securities on said day preceding the second Monday of April, and any indebtedness created in the purchase of such bonds or securities shall not be deducted from the credits under the fourteenth item of this section; but the person making such statement may exhibit to the assessor the property covered by the first nine items of this section, and allow the assessor to fix the value thereof; and in such case the oath of the person making the statement shall be in that regard only that he has fully exhibited the property covered in said nine items."

It is also provided that any person required to list property who shall claim that there is no taxable property within his control which he owns or which he has on account of others, shall be required to make oath to that effect. Persons may be summoned, questioned under oath; and if any person fails to appear, or, appearing, refuses to testify, " he shall be subject to like proceedings and penalties for contempt as a witness in actions pending in the probate court. If a person refuses to list or swear his property to the assessor, the auditor shall add 50% to the amount returned or ascertained, and the amount thus increased shall be the basis of taxation."

In addition to these provisions of the statutes there is what is called a Tax Inquisitor Law, which gives the County Commissioners authority to make a contract with persons who may give information which will result in personal property being placed on the assessment roll. In Hamilton and Cuyahoga counties such informers may be paid 25% of the amount collected, and in the rest of the State 20% of the amount collected. Debts may be deducted from credits, but otherwise there is no exemption because of indebtedness.

In 1893 a Tax Commission was appointed by Governor McKinley—two Democrats and two Republicans—to investigate the whole subject of taxation. In its report the Commission said: "We have in Ohio the most efficient and minute scheme of bringing upon the duplicate all of this class of property which has been devised in any State." After describing the system, the Commission presents numerous illustrations all designed to show that the amount of personal property assessed has rather decreased than increased. In one table it presents the moneys and stocks and bonds returned for taxation in the different city counties of Ohio for the years 1881 and 1892—that is, before and after the passage of the Tax Inquisitor Law. This table shows that in almost every case less money was assessed in 1892 than in 1881, and less stocks and bonds, or a very small increased amount, in spite of the fact that the various cities were increasing at a rapid rate in population and wealth. In the footnote* I present this table as made by the Commission of 1893 with the corresponding figures for 1903. In Cincinnati there is actually less money and less in stocks and bonds assessed in 1903 than in 1881.

Summing up the whole matter the Commission says: "The system as it is actually administered results in debauching the moral sense. It is a school of perjury. It sends large amounts of property into hiding. It drives capital in large quantities from the State. Worst of all, it imposes unjust burdens upon various classes in the community; upon the farmer in the country, all of whose property is taxed because it is tangible; upon the man who is scrupulously honest, and upon the guardian and

---

	MONEY.	STOCKS AND BONDS.
* Hamilton County, 1881	$2,217,868	$2,135,878
Hamilton County, 1892	1,585,375	2,256,223
Hamilton County, 1903	1,193,077	1,399,515
Cuyahoga County, 1881	1,402,322	1,836,654
Cuyahoga County, 1892	1,800,593	2,085,001
Cuyahoga County, 1903	2,385,016	1,823,240
Lucas County, 1881	174,946	51,935
Lucas County, 1892	253,087	176,644
Lucas County, 1903	558,804	218,360
Franklin County, 1881	1,513,965	594,897
Franklin County, 1892	1,094,448	897,080
Franklin County, 1903	1,324,590	408,082
Montgomery County, 1881	1,643,958	610,835
Montgomery County, 1892	1,354,593	485,254
Montgomery County, 1903	1,702,891	257,233
State-at-large, 1881	40,642,949	8,637,850
State-at-large, 1892	38,417,478	10,556,756
State-at-large, 1903	61,492,870	9,856,355

executor and trustee, whose accounts are matters of public record."

For a number of years Ohio has endeavored to amend the Constitution so as to make a reasonable system of taxation possible. So far these amendments have failed because it is necessary to obtain a majority of all the votes cast at an election to pass an amendment to the Constitution. In 1903 an amendment was adopted by the Legislature and submitted to the people. By this amendment the clause for the equal taxation of all property was stricken out and the following language substituted: "The General Assembly shall provide for the raising of all state revenue for all state and local purposes in such manner as it shall deem proper. The subjects of taxation for state and local purposes shall be classified, and the taxation shall be uniform on all subjects of the same class, and shall be just to the subject taxed."

This amendment was prepared by the Ohio State Board of Commerce and was indorsed by the Cincinnati and Cleveland Chambers of Commerce and by 21 other organizations throughout the State. The Republican platform of 1903 declared:

"We favor removing the limitations which prevent a more just system of taxation, so that property can be adequately classified for taxation purposes, and invite the most careful consideration of the amendment for that purpose to be voted upon at the election next November."

The Democratic party, in their platform, declared as follows:

"Taxation: We heartily indorse the constitutional amendment now pending before the people, to be voted upon at the coming election."

The vote upon the amendment was 326,622 in favor and 43,562 opposed. The amendment failed because it did not receive a constitutional majority of all the votes cast at the election. The Ohio State Board of Commerce declares that this amendment will be submitted to the next Legislature, and calls upon the people of the State to give it hearty support.

ILLINOIS.

In the State of Illinois the statutes require personal property to be listed yearly according to the quantity owned on the 1st of May. Persons listing are required to make statement under oath and to deliver to the assessor an itemized schedule of the number, amounts, quantity and quality of all taxable personal property in their possession or under their control. When any person refuses to make and verify the schedule required, it is the assessor's duty to list the property of such person according to his best judgment, and to add a penalty of 50 per cent. to the valuation; the person refusing being subject also to a fine of $200, as for a misdemeanor.

By 1897 this system was a complete wreck in Chicago and was little better in the remainder of the State. Personal property in Chicago amounted to only 13.5 per cent. of the total taxable valuation of all property, and in the remainder of the State it amounted to only 17.7 per cent. Cook County (containing the City of Chicago) in that year had one-third of the total real estate value of the State and only one-sixty-third in value of watches and clocks, one-ninth as much money, one-twenty-second as much value in carriages and wagons, and one-fifty-fifth as much of credits.

Recently all attempts to obey the letter of the law was abandoned in Chicago, and for the tax upon personal property there has been substituted what is practically a gross revenue tax upon business. Professor Commons has described this extra-legal system in the *Review of Reviews*.* It is a striking testimony to the impossibility of enforcing the general property tax in a large city and to the practical nature of the American people, who in this case have managed to work some sort of rough justice while entirely disregarding the letter of the law.

The relation between the assessed value of the various items of personal property classified in Cook County and in the remainder of the State is an object lesson to farmers just as it was in 1897.

MISSOURI CITIES.

Missouri is blessed by the same kind of a listing law as that of Ohio and Illinois. There are only four large cities in the State, and the iniquitous effect of personal property taxation is clearly shown by a comparison between the city counties and the remainder of the State, or between the City of St. Louis and one of the rural counties (1899). In the four city counties personal property amounts to less than 14 per cent. of the total assessed value of real and personal property, while in the remainder of

* February, 1903.

the State it amounts to 28 per cent. In St. Louis personal property amounts to 12 per cent., and in the rural county of Camden it amounts to 30 per cent. of the total. Camden County is an exceedingly good illustration of the way the taxation of personal property affects the farmers. The assessed value of the property in the county is $1,773,076. Of this amount 30 per cent. is personal property, and nearly two-thirds of this personal property by value consists of live stock; that is, over one-sixth of the entire taxable value of Camden County is live stock. Under a severe listing system it is absolutely impossible for farmers to avoid paying taxes on their live stock, and the result is that farmers, as a class, pay vastly more in taxes than they ought to pay. The effect of this upon the cities is indirect, but none the less extremely harmful. The farming industry is discouraged, and country boys are driven to the cities, where their competition reduces the wages of those who are city born.

WEST VIRGINIA.

In West Virginia there are no large cities, and consequently personal property pays a large share of the taxes, averaging for the whole State over 28 per cent. A New York assemblyman once said that the personal property tax worked beautifully in West Virginia, because there is a severe listing system there, and he said that this proved that all the State of New York or any other State needed was to imitate the system of West Virginia. This theory might sound well to one unacquainted with the facts, but, as always, the facts in West Virginia give the lie to any theory of universal taxation.

In Ohio County town lots are more than double the value of farm lands, and personal property pays 25 per cent. of the taxes; while in Harrison County, in which farm lands are six times the value of town lots, personal property pays 36 per cent. of the taxes. In West Virginia a record is kept of the various items of personal property. In Ohio County, which had more than double the real estate value of Harrison County, watches and clocks are assessed at $1,550, while in Harrison County they are assessed at $15,425, or ten times as much. The 27,000 inhabitants of Harrison County have 2,514 watches and clocks (exclusive of those in stock in stores or factories), while the 48,000 inhabitants of Ohio County get along with 34 (according to the assessors). These figures are from the Auditor's report for 1902, and there is no evidence of any improvement since the report of the commission in 1884, which said: "Things have come to such a condition in West Virginia that, as regards paying taxes on this class of property, it is almost as voluntary and is considered pretty much in the same light as donations to a neighboring church or Sunday school."

A special commission on taxation reported in 1902. In their report they advocated the abolition of taxes on intangible property. They said that strong arguments had been presented to them for the entire exemption from taxation of improvements on land, and they recommended that power be given to the municipalities of the State to exempt intangible property, manufacturing plants or all personal property, also to exempt improvements on land in whole or in part.

MASSACHUSETTS.

A commission appointed to inquire into the expediency of revising the tax laws of the State, in their report, issued in 1897, says: "The taxation of personal property in the form of securities and investments is thus a failure. It is incomplete, uncertain, not proportional to the means as between individuals, grossly unequal in its effects in different parts of the State. The experience of Massachusetts in this regard is the same as that of the other States in the Union. Everywhere, without exception, the testimony is that this part of the system of the general property tax is unequal, unsuccessful, often demoralizing to tax officers, always irritating to taxpayers.

"The experience of Massachusetts is the more striking because here the difficulty does not lie mainly in the administration of the tax laws. The assessors are usually honest, competent, zealous. We have heard much of grave abuses, of almost corrupt laxity, in other States, but in this Commonwealth, notwithstanding occasional defections (some of which we have just referred to), the standard of public duty continues to be high, and the cause of failure is not to be found mainly in official dereliction. It lies in the system itself."

A special commission appointed by the Mayor of Boston reported in April, 1891, and said that it would be greatly to the benefit of Boston to abolish personal taxes altogether. On page 24 of their report they said: "In Philadelphia personal property is not doubly taxed; in New York it is seldom doubly taxed;

in Boston the most strenuous efforts are made to collect a double tax upon it. Boston and Massachusetts are both avoided like a house guarded by a savage dog. It is true that one may not be bitten, but it is pleasanter to go where the dog is not so fierce.

"Our system is a scarecrow, and a most efficient one.

"Both capital and men are free in this country; they go where they please.

"Enoch Ensley, of Tennessee, lays down this axiom: 'Never tax anything that would be of value to your State that could and would run away, or that could or would come to you.'

"Untold millions of industrial capital has been warned away from Massachusetts and driven out of it by our oppressive and unreasonable laws, and many a millionaire has feared to come here or left here for the same reason.

"We all know that the value of real estate depends upon the capital employed on it. The more capital there is the more demand for labor. We should seek to attract capital. We should not continue to warn it off and drive it out."

A FAILURE IN NEW JERSEY.

New Jersey testifies to the same effect. A commission was appointed in that State by Governor Griggs to investigate the subject of taxation and reported in 1897. The commission says: "It is now literally true in New Jersey, as in other States, as has been well said by another, that the only ones who now pay honest taxes on personal property are the estates of decedents, widows and orphans, idiots and lunatics. * * * The reports of our State Board of Taxation for 1893, 1894 and 1895 speak of these things and decry them, and like complaints have come to us from many sources."

Then follows a complete table of the counties of the State, with the assessed value of real and personal property and the percentage of taxes paid by each class of property. In speaking of this table the commission said: "It is submitted, this table speaks for itself—is a significant indictment of our present tax laws—and reveals evils and abuses in New Jersey taxation that, together with the foregoing, call for due and early remedies."

MINNESOTA.

Minnesota has the same constitutional provision with reference to taxation that is found in the Ohio Constitution. In 1902 a tax commission made a report, in which they said:* "So

* Report Minnesota Tax Commission, pp. 6 and 7, 1902.

universally is the evasion of the law in the assessment of personal property practiced and so notorious is the fact that much the greater volume of it is unassessed, that its evasion is often regarded a virtue rather than a vice. In few, if any, States is more than 25 per centum of the personal property liable to taxation listed for assessment.

"It necessarily results that, in the enforcement of the law with respect to such property, numerous instances of gross injustice occur. So far as it is reached at all it belongs chiefly to banks, the estates of decedents, insolvents, minors, persons of small means and the comparatively few who conscientiously list their property.

"It has unquestionably given rise to widespread immorality. Men of unquestioned business integrity not only find little difficulty in listing their property far below its real value, but also in making oath to lists which they know to be false.

"It has long been the policy of this State, as well as many other States, to tax mortgages and other forms of credit. Long experience has demonstrated that such a law can at best be but imperfectly enforced. Students of taxation, with scarcely an exception, denounce it as fallacious in principle and a fruitful source of immorality."

In 1902 the Legislature adopted an amendment to the Constitution, but failed to take the advice of their Tax Commission, and made a long, complicated amendment, giving additional power to the Legislature in minor matters, instead of abolishing all restrictions upon the power of the Legislature. This amendment was defeated by the people. This year, 1905, the Legislature has adopted a simple amendment which practically gives all power to the Legislature. The amendment was passed by a Republican Legislature and signed by a Democratic Governor. There is every prospect of its acceptance by the people.

KENTUCKY.

In 1903 Kentucky adopted a constitutional amendment authorizing cities and towns to substitute for the general property tax on personal property, income and license taxes, and in 1904 a law was passed carrying out the provisions of the amendment.

KANSAS.

The necessity for amendment is appreciated in Kansas, as is seen by the Governor's message to the Legislature of 1903. Governor Bailey said: "For many years it has been generally conceded that our present tax law is insufficient for present conditions, crude and inequitable in its operation. Framed thirty-four years ago, when Kansas was a frontier State, and all its property visible and easy of assessment, it is now imperfect and wholly inadequate to meet the changed conditions of society."

CALIFORNIA.

Governor Pardee, of California, in his message to the Legislature in 1903, calls attention to the inequitable working of the California law, a law very similar to that of Minnesota. The Governor said: "The amount of personal property assessed in California is actually less by several millions than it was thirty years ago. As long ago as 1872 the assessors found nearly $220,000,000 worth of personal property. A few years later the assessment had shrunk to a little more than half of that sum. and though there has since been a slow increase, it amounts for the current year to only $200,000,000."

TEXAS.

Texas has a similar restrictive Constitution, and Governor Sayres, in his message in 1903, said: "It is strictly true that the amount of property escaping taxation steadily increases year by year, and that when rendition is made it is so rated as to hardly reach one-third of its true market value."

ONTARIO.

In Canada more progress has been made in improving methods of local taxation than throughout the United States; but until recently the general property tax was in common use. It has lately been abolished in the City of Toronto, largely as a result of the work of the Ontario Assessment Commission, which reported in 1902. In their report they said (page 15): "The conclusion would seem to be that in Ontario, as everywhere else, the direct taxation of personal property generally fails to reach the new kinds of property or wealth which modern civilization has produced. The more comprehensive general property tax which prevails in most of the States of the American Union fails in spite of the most stringent provisions for the discovery of personal property. The various attempts to compel its enforcement by stricter inquiries and greater penalties have only brought a train of moral evils upon the community, without reaching the property intended to be taxed. As Professor Ely has said of it: 'The more you perfect it the worse you make it.' In its application to personal property it has been pronounced to be unequal, capricious in its incidence, replete with incongruities, and its deficiencies of principle are aggravated and exacerbated by its non-enforcement.

"From another entirely different point of view the General Property Tax fails in its intended effect. When taxes are imposed on different classes of persons in proportion to their ability to pay, measured by their wealth, it is with the object that those persons upon whom the tax is laid shall really bear it. If they can shift it to others they are really not taxed. Experience would seem to show that when merchants, lenders of money, insurance companies, and many others are taxed on their capitalized property, the only effect is to raise the price of goods, the rate of interest, premiums, etc., so that the tax really falls upon others, the persons who deal with them."

MARYLAND.

As a member of the Tax Commission of the State of Maryland, Professor Richard T. Ely made a supplementary report in 1888. He says that there is great dissatisfaction with the tax conditions and proceeds:* "This dissatisfaction has increased without interruption up to the present time, and every year renders our existing methods of assessing property and of taxing it more intolerable. The endeavors to improve upon actual methods have been frequent and are daily increasing in frequency, but they usually prove fruitless or render a bad matter worse, because those who make them have failed to go to the root of the evil, which is the system itself. The truth is the existing system is so radically bad, that the more you improve it the worse it becomes. This lies in the nature of things, and nothing any Legislature can do can alter this condition of things. Experience and reason alike teach this, and in my opinion place it beyond controversy for all those who have eyes to see what is passing about them every day of their lives.

* Supplementary report on Taxation, pp. 100, 101 and 104, Richard T. Ely. Report Maryland Tax Commission to the General Assembly, 1888.

"*The Testimony of Experience.*—I have first to remark that the one uniform tax on all property as an exclusive source of revenue, or the chief source—the main feature in direct taxation—never worked well in any modern community or State in the entire civilized world, though it has been tried thousands of times, and although all the mental resources of able men have been employed to make it work well. I have read diligently the literature of finance to find an example, but in vain, and lest this should not be sufficiently trustworthy, I have made it my business, in my capacity as Tax Commissioner, to visit typical States and cities and to make inquiries in person, of citizens as well as officials entrusted with the administration of the laws. I have visited Charleston, South Carolina; Savannah, Atlanta and Augusta, Georgia; Columbus, Ohio; Madison, Wisconsin; Toronto, Montreal and Quebec, Canada; and the result has been abundantly to confirm all that I have said about the impracticability of the one uniform tax on real and personal property."

Theory of the General Property Tax.

The theory of the General Property Tax requires the equal taxation of all property by the same rule. Out of the attempt to put this theory in practice has grown a further theory that in order to be equal taxation must be equally imposed on all property. Experience shows that the practice antedated the theory. To carry out this theory all property must be assessed and taxed at its true value, and it assumes that the pressure of taxation shall be equal upon all forms of property just as the pressure of the air is equal upon all tangible objects.

If the theory ever could work anywhere, it could only work in a community absolutely isolated from all the rest of the world. Under conditions as they actually exist a few comparisons between different kinds of property will be sufficient to show the impossibility of obtaining the conditions under which alone the theory could work with any degree of perfection. One who invests in real estate in any city pays a price based upon existing conditions, and in effect buys an annual income; for example, he pays the sum of $10,000 for property which will yield $500 a year. If the property should yield only $400 he would pay no more than $8,000 for it. He buys with reference to known local conditions. On the other hand, if one buys railroad bonds he must pay a price fixed by world markets, and if he is so fortunate as to secure safe bonds that pay 5 per cent., $10,000 will buy an income of $500 in the absence of any taxation. If the bonds are taxed 2½ per cent., his income is but $250, instead of the sum of $500, which he would get from an investment in real estate.

If all retail merchants in a city are taxed equally the tax will be added to the price at which they sell their goods, and they will be able to make the usual profit upon capital invested in such business. A manufacturer who makes articles for export can only sell in competition with manufacturers in other States and countries, and taxes levied on him in excess of taxes upon a similar business elsewhere reduce his profits, and may reduce them to such an extent as to force him to remove to a more favorable place.

If money is invested in a mortgage in any State in which mortgages are taxable (except California, Oregon and, after July 1st, New York), the investment is not based upon the equal taxation of all mortgages in that State, but is made in competition with money sent from outside the State for investment there.

Instances showing the impossibility of treating all alike by a general property tax imposed equally on all property might be multiplied indefinitely. These examples suffice to show the utter lack of uniformity produced by a so-called "equal tax." The theory has been abandoned and a modern theory takes its place, which is that property must be classified according to its nature, and taxed or exempted from taxation in accordance with justice, expediency and practicability. This theory has received in effect the indorsement of one of our most thoughtful bodies. In the case of Pacific Express Co. *vs.* Seibert (142 U. S., 351), the United States Supreme Court said:

"This Court has repeatedly laid down the doctrine that diversity of taxation, both in respect to the amount imposed and the various species of property selected either for bearing its burdens or for being exempt from them, is not inconsistent with a perfect uniformity and equality of taxation in the proper sense of those terms; and that a system which imposes the same tax upon every species of property, irrespective of its nature, condition or class, will be destructive of the principle of uniformity and equality in taxation and of a just adaptation of property to its burdens."

What Shall We Do in the City of New York.

The evidence presented could be multiplied many fold, but it seems ample to demonstrate that every effort should be put forth to get rid of the general property tax, and that any attempt to patch it up will only make a bad matter worse and render the task more difficult. It cannot be doubted that in the City of New York the public mind is ready for great changes, and that if we had the power we would speedily effect a vast improvement. If we should propose almost anything to take the place of the tax on personal property it is certain we should array a larger body of opinion against our proposal than in favor of it. The next step is to secure the power to change.

In suggesting that we should secure the power to change we are not proposing anything new, but a remedy which has been tried with success elsewhere, and has been recommended here on many occasions and in several forms. It was recommended by our great Tax Commissioner, George H. Andrews, in a memorial to the Legislature in 1874. In the course of his address to the Assembly Committee on Ways and Means Mr. Andrews said: "The effect of the present laws for assessing personal property is disastrous to the owners of real estate, inasmuch as many of our best citizens remove to the States already enumerated to avoid the operation of our tax laws. The real estate of the State needs for its development and prosperity residents, capital and business. These are the elements which, coursing through the veins of the community, give it life and health. Without these real estate must droop and languish, but with these trade must flourish, mechanics find employment, stores and tenements be fully occupied, the farmer find a ready market for his produce, and the sunshine of prosperity gladden every heart and lighten every burden.

"Under the operation of the present laws real estate must continue to bear more and more of the burden of taxation, and also suffer heavily because those laws, instead of attracting, scare away residents, capital and business."

In his message to the Board of Aldermen in 1888 Mayor Hewitt recommended that the City should have power to abolish personal taxes, and said: "The abolition of personal taxes in this city would attract to it the capital of the whole world. We are now the centre of exchanges on the Western Continent, but in a few years we should be the clearing house for the commerce of the globe. * * * Any proposition to impose taxation upon what people or corporations owe, instead of what they own, is absolutely unsound, and it is difficult to understand by what process of reasoning this policy is advocated. According to the conclusions of the best financial authorities actual property should alone be taxed. Evidences of debt should never be taxed, because, as a rule, they only represent property which has already been taxed. No sounder system of taxation for local or State purposes can be devised than that which practically puts the tax upon tangible and visible property, and upon public franchises which have an actual cash value, as shown by their earning power."

In 1901 the New York Chamber of Commerce endorsed a bill designed to give The City of New York the power to make changes in its system of taxation, by doing two things. First: It provides that the proportion of revenue The City of New York shall pay to the State and that the other counties of the State shall pay to the State, shall be based upon the amount of revenue derived locally. This does away with the necessity for uniformity throughout the State and makes possible a grant of power to the local authorities to make changes in the local system. The bill further contains a section conferring this grant of power:

"Sec. 4*a*. Other property may be exempted from taxation, or the assessment upon the same reduced, as provided in this section, but such exemption or reduction of assessment shall have uniform operation throughout the county or city in which it is made, and shall not be made on the ground of ownership. Within any county such property shall be exempt from taxation or the assessment upon the same reduced in such manner as the board of supervisors of such county shall from time to time prescribe. Within any incorporated city, extending over the whole of any one county or over more than one county, such property shall be exempt from taxation, or the assessment upon the same reduced in such manner, as the board of aldermen of such city shall from time to time prescribe. Nothing contained in any special act, or the act incorporating any city or village, shall affect the validity or operation of any such exemption or reduction of assessment. The provisions of this section shall not affect section four nor articles nine, ten, fourteen and fifteen of this chapter, nor any other general law of the state."

The bill is printed in full as an appendix to this report. It has been endorsed by the Chamber of Commerce of the State of New York, the State Commerce Convention, Board of Trade and Transportation, Merchants' Association, West End Association, United Real Estate Owners' Associations, Business Men's Association of Cohoes, and other associations of business men, the Central Federated Union, the Building Trades Council and many other labor organizations.

It will be seen that provision is made not only for the exemption of property from taxation altogether, but for a reduction of the rate of assessment if that shall be deemed desirable. It might be that instead of abolishing the tax on some forms of property entirely, it would be deemed wise to reduce the rate, and if the experience of Pennsylvania and Connecticut is worth anything, it is demonstrated that a smaller tax on certain forms of personal property will produce a considerably larger revenue than a larger tax. Again, the main objection to the abolition of the tax upon personal property is that the rate would be increased upon real estate, and thus tend to check improvements and make the building of homes for the people more costly. The power to reduce the assessment on any form of property would permit a reduction of the rate of assessment upon dwellings and other improvements. This would entirely counteract any tendency to check the erection of buildings, and indeed would encourage their erection.

So long as a tax on land does not increase faster than the value of the land increases, it is not a burden upon the owner. Professor Ely says:*

"When the tax on the value of land is liable to comparatively slight variation, and is something which can be calculated upon as a fixed and unalterable fact, it partakes of the nature of a charge upon the land, and to this extent it may be said to amount simply to partial public ownership. A farmer owns, let us say, one hundred acres of ground purchased for $10,000, but a mortgage for $5,000 rests on it because he was able to pay only one-half of the purchase money. He feels the burden of taxation and groans under it, yet he should reflect that he would be no better off if his land had never been taxed, for in that case he would have been obliged to pay so much more for it, and instead

* Taxation in American states and cities, Richard T. Ely, pp. 246, 247 and 248, 1888.

of being $5,000 in debt, he would owe, perhaps, $7,000. I recently purchased a house, and in deciding how much I was willing to pay, I took into consideration the taxes. If the house had been exempt from taxation, I would have been asked more for it, and would have been willing to give proportionately more. How, then, can I say that I am really bearing any burden at all? I simply pay the public annually for its claim on my property, and if this claim should be released, it would be equivalent to a present to me. Of course, if the rate of taxation is raised, it amounts to this, that the claim on my property is raised and the value of the part owned by the public increases. The more invariable and permanent taxes are, the larger the extent to which the above principle can be applied. * * *

"Apart from this, land is visible, easily valued, and permanent in its location, and these qualities render it specially suitable for taxation. The following reasons have also been given for a tax on real estate, more particularly on land: Land derives an increased value from public security and from public works, and taxes are expended chiefly for these two purposes. This is so true with reference to public improvements that many of our growing cities have become embarrassed by expenditure made at the solicitation of land owners, particularly on occasion of 'booms,' and not, as popularly imagined, by the moneyless rabble. An instance recently occurred in Buffalo, where large expenditures were forced upon the people by real estate owners, and against the protest of at least some of the workingmen. A second reason is that the tax may be considered as a return to the community for the rights which it has surrendered in what was once common property.

"All assessors should be by law especially directed to assess to the last dollar of its true value all real estate held for speculative purposes. There is a common and iniquitous practice, which I have observed everywhere in my investigations, of undervaluing land held for a rise, and not used at all, or used only for some unnatural purpose, as when city lots are utilized as cow pastures. Such land is occasionally actually valued as farm land. Thus men, without a stroke of work, and even while obstructing the natural growth of cities, see their property steadily increase in value, and this is solely due to the industry and thrift of their fellows."

SUMMARY.

In view of the experience of foreign countries and those American States which have employed the most thorough and stringent means of taxing personal property, it is plain that the system is wrong in principle and should be abolished; that any plan for enforcing the law more efficiently by repealing the provision allowing the deduction of debts from personal assets, by subjecting additional property of non-residents to taxation, or by requiring sworn statements from taxpayers, will increase the injustice now done to individuals and work against the interest of real estate owners by driving away persons and property which alone give value to city real estate. By increasing the amount collected for a time it will render the abolition of the tax more difficult.

Personal property amounts to 13% of all the property assessed in The City of New York, but over one-third of the personal taxes are not collected, so that in fact personal property, assessed for the general property tax, only pays about 8% of the taxes. It would be greatly to the advantage of all the people of the city to abolish the tax at once and entirely. In view of the relation of the City to the State this is impossible, and I therefore recommend to the Commission for their approval the annexed bill for the Apportionment of State Taxes and for Local Option in Taxation.

LAWSON PURDY.

Appendix.

An Act to amend the Tax Law by providing for the apportionment of State Taxes and for local option in taxation.

The People of the State of New York, represented in Senate and Assembly, do enact as follows:

Section 1. The Tax Law is hereby amended by adding thereto, after Section 4, the following section:

§ 4*a*. Other property may be exempted from taxation, or the assessment upon the same reduced, as provided in this section, but such exemption or reduction of assessment shall have uniform operation throughout the county or city in which it is made, and shall not be made on the ground of ownership. Within any county such property shall be exempt from taxation, or the assessment upon the same reduced in such manner, as the board of supervisors of such county shall from time to time prescribe. Within any incorporated city, extending over the whole of any one county or over more than one county, such property shall be exempt from taxation, or the assessment upon the same reduced in such manner, as the board of aldermen of such city shall from time to time prescribe. Nothing contained in any special act, or the act incorporating any city or village, shall affect the validity or operation of any such exemption or reduction of assessment. The provisions of this section shall not affect section four nor articles nine, ten, fourteen and fifteen of this chapter, nor any other general law of the State.*

Section 2. Section 171 of the Tax Law is hereby amended by adding thereto the following:

Ninth. Obtain annually from the financial officer or other officer or person charged with the custody and disbursement of any funds of each tax district of the state a report of the amount of gross revenue of each tax district for the preceding calendar year and the sources of such revenue; and for this purpose such local officer of each tax district, at the expense of such district, shall furnish such information in such form as may be required by the state board of tax commissioners. Neglect or refusal

* Section four, of this Chapter, provides that certain property shall be exempt from taxation. Articles nine, ten, fourteen, and fifteen deal with the taxation, for State purposes, of corporations; transfers of property by will, by the intestate laws of the State or in expectation of death; the tax on sales of stock; and on mortgages.

to file a true and correct report in the office of the state board of tax commissioners at the time and in the form required by the board is a misdemeanor, the making and filing of a report containing a willful misstatement is a felony.

Tenth. Classify and file, according to tax districts, the reports of gross revenue which they obtain from local officers.

Eleventh. Examine the reports of gross revenue filed with them; and tabulate the results of such examination, so as to show summarily, and in separate tables, for each tax district, for each county and for all the counties of the State, and for each calendar year, (1) the gross revenue, (2) the sources of such revenue, (3) any other results which they think it for the public interest to exhibit. They shall present a report of the results of such examination to the state board of apportionment at its meeting on the first Tuesday in September.

"Tax district," as used in this section and in section 173 of this chapter, means a political subdivision of the state, having a board of assessors, or an assessor or officer, authorized to assess property therein for taxation for state, county, city, village, school, highway, or any other purpose whatever, or having an officer or officers authorized to sign warrants for the collection of taxes.

"Gross revenue," as used in this section, and in section 173 of this chapter, means the total sum of money received by any tax district for public purposes, and the value, at the rate of commutation allowed by law, of work performed for the tax district without compensation under a requirement of law. But it does not include assessments for local improvements, money borrowed, money received as interest on any obligation of the tax district owned by said district or held in trust for it by any board or officer, or so much of the revenue from sales to private users of water, gas, electricity, or other industrial service as represents the cost thereof.

For the purpose of this section, and of section 173 of this chapter, the city of New York shall be deemed to be one county.

SECTION 3. Section 173, of the Tax Law, is hereby amended so as to read as follows:

§ 173. State board of [*equalization*] apportionment powers and duties.

The commissioners of the land office and the three commissioners of taxes shall constitute the state board of [*equalization*] apportionment. The state board of [*equalization*] apportionment shall meet in the city of Albany on the first Tuesday in September in each year [*for the purpose of examining and revising the valuations of real and personal property of the several counties as returned to the board of tax commissioners, and shall fix the aggregate amount of assessment for each county, upon which the controller shall compute the state tax. Such board may increase or diminish the aggregate valuations of real property in any county by adding or deducting such sum as in its opinion may be just and necessary to produce a just relation between the valuations of real property in the state. But it shall, in no instance, reduce the aggregate valuations of all the counties below the aggregate valuations thereof as so returned*] and, at such meeting, shall ascertain and determine the percentage of state tax each county shall pay, by dividing the sum of the gross revenue, for the preceding calendar year, of each county including all the tax districts within the county, by the sum of the gross revenue of all the tax districts of the state for the same year. The comptroller shall immediately ascertain from this [*assessment*] determination of the percentage of state tax which each county shall pay, a copy of which shall be transmitted to him, the [*proportion*] amount of state tax each county shall pay, and mail a statement of the amount to the county clerk and to the chairman and clerk of the board of supervisors of each county.

SECTION 4. This act shall take effect October first, 1906.

EXPLANATION.—*Matter underscored ——— is new; matter in brackets [ ] is old law to be omitted.*

ADVISORY COMMISSION

ON

TAXATION AND FINANCE

REPORT

OF

COMMITTEE ON TAXATION AND REVENUE

ON

PERSONAL PROPERTY TAXATION

DECEMBER, 1906

Report on Personal Property Taxation.

HON. GEORGE B. MCCLELLAN,
Mayor of The City of New York,
City Hall, New York:

DEAR SIR—At an early day a special tax commission will report to the Legislature and its recommendations may be of vital importance to The City of New York. As the greatest city of the United States, New York has the most complex and delicate commercial and financial organization. It is moreover in very close touch with other States to which persons and property can easily withdraw if tax burdens are unwisely imposed. Under these circumstances the people of New York are all deeply concerned in the taxation of movable property.

The personal property tax is a farce. It falls inequitably upon the comparatively few who are caught. The burden it imposes upon production is out of all proportion to the revenue it produces. Year after year state and local assessing boards have denounced it as impracticable in its workings and unjust in its results. These recommendations have for the most part passed unheeded or have led to ineffectual attempts to bolster up the law. It is time the situation was faced squarely, and the tax in its present form abolished.

Manufacturers and merchants should have at least as much relief as has been given financiers. The state has made flat taxes for banks and trust companies and for mortgages, lower in rate than the taxes to which such property was formerly liable. What is even more important, these taxes fall upon each class with certainty and without discrimination. It is generally admitted that the annual tax on mortgages of one-half of one per cent. was a check to building and an undue burden upon improvers. What then must be the effect on trade of taxes upon commerce and manufactures, which are one and a half per cent. in this city, and in other cities of the state still greater?

The City of New York is fast becoming the greatest city of the world in population and in wealth. But this is in spite of foolish tax laws and not because of wise ones. Its growth has been due largely to its location, and its supremacy is financial rather than industrial. Its industries and its trade should be relieved from the handicap now laid upon them, and the commercial growth of the city should keep pace with its development on other lines. The manufacturers who go to other states should be encouraged to come and to stay in the city, or at least in the State of New York.

Millions of dollars are being spent upon improved transportation facilities, so that our fast increasing population can find proper homes. While we are justly proud of the city's growth, still we must remember that it is one-sided. The increase is largely of clerical and office help, working in Manhattan and seeking homes in the other boroughs. If the same kind of growth continues, it is inevitable that a great many more workers will seek homes in New Jersey. If we had our fair quota of mechanics and factory hands we would double and treble the value of our lands, and the increase in population would be more evenly distributed, for such workers would reside near their employment and within the state. The area within our own city limits could contain many times our present population, and give room to many times its present industries. While it is true that land on Manhattan Island is too valuable to be used for most kinds of heavy manufacturing, there is plenty of low-priced land available elsewhere within the city limits. With Long Island connected by rail with the main land and with improved facilities for freightage by water, there is no reason but taxation why Queens County should not become as thriving a manufacturing centre as Newark.

The State of New Jersey in its Industrial Directory, setting forth the advantages offered to manufacturers, assures them that "Everywhere throughout the state the policy pursued in taxing manufacturing plants is, very wisely, a most liberal one. The value placed on such property by assessors is often no greater than 25 per cent. and seldom above 33 per cent. of its true cost." This year the policy of assessing real estate at full value in New Jersey has reduced the ratio of personal property assessed to the total assessment, from 16 per cent. to 10 per cent. As a result of this large exemption to manufacturing industries the railroad lines from Jersey City to Trenton and Paterson are becoming a continuous row of factories. The seven counties adjacent to New York have increased 16 per cent. in population in the last five years.

In that period the capital invested in manufactures in New Jersey has increased 50 per cent., and the value of the annual products 40 per cent.; while in The City of New York the invested capital increased only 22 per cent. and the products only 30 per cent.

Pennsylvania, that has never taxed the goods or other personal property of manufacturers, is increasing its capital and products faster than New York, especially in the districts outside the larger cities. A very large proportion of industries in The City of New York are so small as to escape taxation, and it is the aggregate value of their products that makes this the greatest manufacturing city of the United States.

If the personal property tax has not been so great a handicap upon merchants as upon manufacturers, this is because the merchants have more readily evaded it. If it could be thoroughly enforced our merchants would have to increase prices and so lose a large part of their trade, or their profits would be decreased so that many of them would be driven elsewhere. But to the extent to which it is enforced the tax upon merchandise hinders commerce. It falls most heavily upon the most conscientious, and thus penalizes the type of merchant upon whom must rest the reputation of the city for business integrity. We recognize the folly of those European cities which by octroi duties upon merchandise increase the cost of living to their inhabitants, but we still endure a system of taxation, which, though more indirect, just as surely increases the cost of goods to the consumer.

So far as the personal property tax attempts to reach intangible forms of wealth, its administration is so comical as to have become a by-word. In practice it has come to be merely a requisition by the board of assessors upon leading citizens for such donations as assessors think should be made, and is paid as assessed, or reduced, according as the citizen agrees with the estimate of the assessor. Such a method of collecting revenue would be a serious menace to democratic institutions were it not so generally recognized as a howling farce.

But it is not a farce to those who are fully assessed. These are chiefly the widows and orphans who are caught when their property is listed in the probate court, and the small investors who are not skillful enough to make non-taxable investments. The tax of 1½ per cent. is equivalent to an income tax of 25 per cent. on a 6 per cent. investment. A general income tax of 10 per cent. would create a revolution—yet we take a quarter of their income or more from the most helpless class in the community.

The attempt to assess all forms of property by one method and tax them at one rate is unsuited to modern conditions. It was long ago abandoned in Europe and has been modified in this State. The city should have the power to make further alterations and to classify property for taxation, subject only to the restriction that taxes shall be uniform upon all property of the same class. The modifications that it may be necessary and wise to make need not now be discussed. The essential matter is that we recognize the inequalities of the present system and obtain the legal authority to change it.

Whatever may be the economic merits or defects of the State system of special taxes, there is no longer need for the State to dictate to any community the method of raising its local revenues. The abolition of the direct State tax upon real and personal property removes the only practical objection to home rule in taxation.

Your Commission respectfully represents that this question is of immediate importance to the City and presents for your consideration the desirability of bringing the matter to the attention of the Governor and State Legislature.

ADVISORY COMMISSION

ON

TAXATION AND FINANCE

REPORT

ON

THE CITY DEBT IN ITS RELATION TO THE CONSTITUTIONAL LIMIT OF INDEBTEDNESS, CONTAINING A PROPOSED AMENDMENT TO SECTION 10 OF ARTICLE VIII OF THE STATE CONSTITUTION

APRIL, 1907

Hon. George B. McClellan, *Mayor:*

Sir—Among the questions referred by you to this Commission was that of the relation of the City debt to the constitutional limitation on municipal indebtedness. Section 10 of article VIII. of the State Constitution, so far as it relates to municipal indebtedness, reads as follows:

> " No county or city shall be allowed to become indebted for any purpose or in any manner to an amount which, including existing indebtedness, shall exceed ten per centum of the assessed valuation of the real estate of such county or city subject to taxation, as it appeared by the assessment-rolls of said county or city on the last assessment for State or county taxes prior to the incurring of such indebtedness; and all indebtedness in excess of such limitation, except such as may now exist, shall be absolutely void, except as herein otherwise provided. No county or city whose present indebtedness exceeds ten per centum of the assessed valuation of its real estate subject to taxation, shall be allowed to become indebted in any further amount until such indebtedness shall be reduced within such limit. This section shall not be construed to prevent the issuing of certificates of indebtedness or revenue bonds issued in anticipation of the collection of taxes for amounts actually contained, or to be contained, in the taxes for the year when such certificates or revenue bonds are issued and payable out of such taxes.
>
> " Nor shall this section be construed to prevent the issue of bonds to provide for the supply of water; but the term of the bonds issued to provide the supply of water shall not exceed twenty years, and a sinking fund shall be created on the issuing of the said bonds for their redemption, by raising annually a sum which will produce an amount equal to the sum of the principal and interest of said bonds at their maturity. All certificates of indebtedness or revenue bonds issued in anticipation of the collection of taxes, which are not retired within five years after their date of issue, and bonds issued to provide for the supply of water, and any debt hereafter incurred by any portion or part of a city, if there shall be any such debt, shall be included in ascertaining the power of the city to become otherwise indebted;

> except that debts incurred by The City of New York after the first day of January, nineteen hundred and four, to provide for the supply of water, shall not be so included. Whenever the boundaries of any city are the same as those of a county, or when any city shall include within its boundaries more than one county, the power of any county wholly included within such city to become indebted shall cease, but the debt of the county, heretofore existing, shall not, for the purposes of this section, be reckoned as a part of the city debt."

Prior to consolidation this limitation worked no inconvenience in the financing of the City's public works. In fact, it may be said that prior to 1898 no Comptroller ever concerned himself with this constitutional provision; for the margin between the City's net debt and the constitutional limit thereof was generally believed to be so large that it was hardly regarded as possessing more than an academic interest, until the litigation preceding the building of the Manhattan-Bronx subway and the debt burdens of consolidation combined to make its problems really vital and urgent of solution. Since 1898, however, the financial officers of the City have continually been forced to appropriate and to administer with constant attention to this provision of the constitution. There have been times when City improvements have had to be postponed until by legislation or by increased real estate assessments the City was placed in a position legally to incur further indebtedness. An example of such relief by legislation may be found in chapter 630 of the Laws of 1900.

The Charter Revision Commission of 1900 recommended to the Legislature that the Constitution be amended by providing that debts incurred by The City of New York after the first day of January, nineteen hundred and four, to provide for the supply of water, should not be included in ascertaining the power of the City to become otherwise indebted, and this amendment to the Constitution was approved by vote of the people in November, 1905. It was believed at the time this exception was made that it was not only necessary, because of the large expenditures (now estimated at $161,000,000) required to furnish the City with an additional and adequate water supply, but that it could also be made safely from the financial point of view because experience has shown that the ownership and operation of water works has been a source of net income rather than of expense.

The vast increase both in area and population of The City of New York during the last ten years has brought with it most important problems (especially those relating to transportation), the necessity for solving which becomes more insistent every year. No such solution is possible without the expenditure of large amounts of money on capital account as well as by way of current expenditure.

The determination of the question, how to make possible the necessary capital expenditure within the limitation prescribed by our constitution, is one of the most important subjects which has been submitted to this Commission for its consideration. For it is claimed that notwithstanding the recent amendment of the Constitution relating to water bonds issued since 1904, the present constitutional provision is not broad enough or elastic enough to give the City that free hand in dealing with the problems before it which is necessary to their proper solution. In order to approach this question intelligently it is necessary to ascertain, first, what, under the present law, will be the margin between the City debt and the constitutional limit thereof for the next few years; and, secondly, what indebtedness the City will probably be obliged to incur during the same period.

First—*Present Margin of Debt-incurring Capacity.*

The following is a summary of the City debt as stated by the Department of Finance as of January 1, 1907:

Net funded debt falling within the terms of the constitutional limitation	$437,771,239 72
Net contract indebtedness	57,346,337 36
Indebtedness for lands acquired	17,109,785 15
Indebtedness for judgments (estimated)	2,000,000 00
Revenue bonds	30,295,000 00
Total indebtedness	$544,522,362 23
10 per cent. of assessed valuation of real estate	573,848,724 50
Balance	$29,326,362 27
Proceeds of bond sales unapportioned	1,816,856 46
Margin available January 1, 1907	$31,143,218 73

The foregoing statement requires some comment.

The item of revenue bonds in the above statement, aggregating $30,295,000, represents bond issues of $20,155,000 in 1905 and 1906 in anticipation of the collection of taxes of the years 1902, 1903 and 1904 and issues of $10,140,000 in 1906 in anticipation of the collection of taxes of the year 1905. Some of these bonds have been redeemed since January 1; more will be redeemed in the near future; but under the City's financial methods such redemption can only take place at the expense of special and trust accounts. While the amount of such revenue bonds outstanding January 1, 1907, was exceptionally large, it still falls short of the estimated amount of uncollectible taxes—$36,000,000—for which the Board of Estimate and Apportionment have authorized the issue of corporate stock under the provisions of chapter 208, Laws of 1906. Sooner or later these latter bonds must be issued, and when issued, this item of liability (of capital account to current revenue) will appear for the first time in the City's debt statement. It follows, therefore, that while the above statement of the City's debt comes nearer to representing the City's true condition of indebtedness than any similar statement previously issued, nevertheless (as we are now endeavoring to deal with future conditions) it would be better to go still further, and, on the principle of assuming that to be done which will have to be done, make the further deduction of $5,705,000 from the foregoing margin—this figure representing the difference between the aggregate of the Revenue Bonds of the years 1902 and 1905, inclusive, outstanding January 1, 1907, and the amount of Corporate Stock authorized to be issued by the Board of Estimate and Apportionment to make good the deficiency in the City Treasury, caused by arrears of uncollectible taxes. Making this deduction gives us an assumed margin of indebtedness on January 1, 1907, of $25,438,218.73.

The liability given in the above statement as accruing for lands acquired for public purposes and not yet paid for is almost entirely estimated. The obligations accrue when the City becomes vested with the title to the property, which may occur before payments are actually made for the same. The original estimate of the liability is based on tax valuations and thereafter, as the condemnation proceedings progress, information is obtained from the Law Department as to the values appraised by the experts in the proceedings. The actual obligation for the property is not determined until the awards are reported. It is the experience of the City's financial officers that the preliminary estimates of liability covered in the debt statement are invariably below the actual cost. On the other hand, it may be said that the debt statements prepared by the Comptroller's Office include certain contract and land liabilities for water purposes which are not now required to be included in estimating the City's debt margin, which liabilities probably aggregate not less than five millions of dollars. This factor of understatement of the City's debt-incurring capacity may therefore be treated as an approximately equal offset to the general underestimate of liability for lands taken in condemnation proceedings—the net result of which would be to leave practically undisturbed the figure of debt margin above given, i. e., $25,438,-218.73.

SECOND—*Factors Enlarging the City's Future Debt-incurring Capacity*

(*a*) The City's debt-incurring capacity is enlarged each year by ten per cent. of the increase, if any, of the assessed valuation of real estate. Ten per cent. of the increases of the assessed valuation of the past three years has been as follows:

1904	$26,399,295 30
1905	20,595,852 20
1906	51,698,494 40
Average for three years..........	$32,897,880 63

It is estimated that the increase in real estate assessments for 1907 will be about $500,000,000, ten per cent. of which would be $50,000,000. It is to be borne in mind, however, that the real estate assessments in this City have of recent years been constantly approaching more and more nearly the theoretical limit of one hundred per cent., or full valuation; also, that the past few years have been years of great prosperity and enhancing values of real estate.

It does not seem to your Commission that in estimating such increases in future years a higher average than thirty million dollars should be assumed for this item. This is, of course, merely a matter of opinion and can be nothing more. It is scarcely conceivable, however, that even under the stress of necessity the Department of Taxes and Assessments could in the next five years maintain an annual increase in real estate assessments as great as those of 1906 and 1907.

(*b*) Another source of increase is that produced by the redemption of debt from annual taxation directly and from local assessments. This will amount in the years 1907-1911, inclusive, to about $5,500,000, or an average of $1,100,000 annually.

(*c*) The margin of indebtedness is also increased by reason of the increase in the Sinking Funds of the City. These funds are available for redemption of debt falling due, and when not so applied may be used for investment in issues of Corporate Stock. Either transaction adds to the City's debt-incurring power. The average yearly increase in the Sinking Funds during the past three years would appear to be about eleven million, three hundred and fifty thousand dollars, and for the immediate future may be reckoned at an amount not exceeding twelve million dollars per annum. If we add this to the increase in tax valuations, and the annual average of $1,100,000 derived from direct redemption of debt from taxation and assessments, we have an average annual increase in the available margin of indebtedness of $43,100,000. In five years this would amount to $215,500,000, which, added to the present margin, would make a debt-incurring capacity during the next five years of $240,938,218.73.

THIRD—*Probable Future Indebtedness to be Incurred*

Some light may be thrown on this subject by examining the actual bond issues during the past five years, which have been as follows:

1902	$29,601,958 19	
1903	43,022,919 42	
1904	81,825,742 87	
1905	41,210,934 23	
1906	57,052,174 58	
Total	$252,713,729 29	
Deducting water bonds	25,026,100 00	
	$227,687,629 29	
Yearly average		$45,537,525 86

It has not been the custom of the City to issue bonds immediately after their authorization by the Board of Estimate and

Apportionment. They are issued only from time to time, as money is required for actual disbursement on account of public improvements. Long before the actual issuing of the bonds, therefore, contracts may have been entered into and certified to by the Comptroller which have created present indebtedness within the purview of the Constitution. It follows, therefore, that a more reliable criterion than the foregoing statement will be obtained by considering the estimated amount of new debt (not merely funded debt, but all constitutional "indebtedness") incurred during each of the past five years (excluding debt for water purposes incurred since January 1, 1904), as shown in part by the communication of the Comptroller to the Board of Estimate and Apportionment, dated December 6, 1904, which appears to be as follows:

1902	$32,364,980 05	
1903	52,792,139 75	
1904	49,339,924 95	
1905	62,920,260 63	
1906	69,172,912 99	
Total	$266,590,218 37	
Average		$53,318,043 67

The bond issues of the immediate future cannot be regarded as wholly subject to the discretionary control of the Board of Estimate and Apportionment. The welfare of the City imperatively demands that certain classes of improvements shall within certain limits be carried on—among which may be mentioned the acquisition of new school sites and the erection of new school houses; opening, paving and repaving streets; constructing sewers, etc. For other purposes, such as parks and public buildings, a determination to economize might succeed in materially curtailing the extent of future bond issues, and in view of the present difficulty of selling City bonds, it is fairly a subject for consideration whether a certain retrenchment in municipal expenditure in line with the proposed economies of general corporate management throughout the country resulting from the present strain on credits and borrowings, will not soon enforce itself as a result of natural financial laws. In dealing with such uncertain factors as these, it may be said that one man's guess is as good as another's.

But we know of no better starting point in dealing with this subject than to treat future developments as likely to proceed upon the same lines as indicated by past experience. It should be remembered also that the City is already committed to the carrying out and completion of many improvements costing a vast sum of money, which could not now be abandoned or unduly delayed, no matter how great might be the desire to retrench. For example, it is not likely that the expenditures necessary to complete the new bridges over the East River and the approaches necessary therefor will fall far short of the expenditure already incurred for these purposes. The City is practically committed to a large future expenditure for the new Bellevue Hospital. The expensive site and building for the new Court House on Union Square, which is at least a possibility, may cost twenty milions or more. Among other contemplated projects may be mentioned the Sea Side Park at Rockaway, the Brooklyn Bridge terminal, a new municipal building for Brooklyn, the Riverside drive extension and the Hudson Memorial Bridge; the cost involved in removing the New York Central tracks from Eleventh avenue and the very large proposed expenditures by the Dock Department, for which a requisition for the issue of twenty-nine million dollars of bonds has already been made. When these are considered in connection with such regularly recurring annual expenditures from bond sales as those required for new school sites and school houses, opening, paving, repaving and sewering streets, small parks, police and fire sites and station houses and other municipal buildings, it will be seen that unless a high degree of conservatism is exercised, the indebtedness which is likely to be incurred in the near future will scarcely fall short of that incurred in the last five years, or $266,590,218.37. This would amount to about twenty-five million dollars more than permitted by our estimate of the debt-incurring capacity accruing to the City within that period—it being borne in mind, however, that this estimate of future indebtedness allows for a liability for rapid transit purposes equal to that incurred during the past five years.

If for the sake of argument the annual increase of assessed valuations of real estate be assumed to be three hundred and fifty millions, instead of three hundred millions, for each of the next five years, the result would be a theoretical ability to carry out such a programme of public improvements by entirely exhausting the debt margin; if the annual increase be assumed to be $400,-

000,000, there would be a surplus of $25,000,000, and on the basis of an annual increase of $500,000,000 there would be a surplus of $75,000,000.

To review the situation, therefore, it would seem that one of three alternatives must be accepted: Either (1) the City must enter into a period of enforced economy in the way of capital expenditure, reaching even so far as the complete abandonment of such public improvements as are not to be regarded as absolutely essential; and a severe retrenchment in regard to even such important needs as school houses and street improvements; or (2) assessed valuations must be forced upwards to a degree which your Commission can but regard as unnatural and likely to result in hardship and injustice; or (3) provision should be made for an amendment to the Constitution increasing the City's power to incur debt.

Your Commission has approached this last alternative with great reluctance. We are fully aware of the enormous increase which has taken place in the last ten years in the City's funded debt, and we do not seek to minimize the ever increasing cost at which the City has utilized its credit—a cost which has increased sixty per cent. in less than twenty years—*i. e.*, from the two and one-half per cent. bonds sold above par in 1889, to the four per cent. bonds of to-day, which are barely salable at the same price.

But on principle, and looking solely to the reasons which led to the insertion in our State Constitution (as well as in those of many other States) of the provision limiting municipal indebtedness, we can find no objection to such an amendment as we intend to suggest.

The chief purpose of this constitutional provision is to prevent cities from imposing too great a burden of debt upon their taxpayers, present and future. What constitutes the burden of debt? Solely the interest charge, and in the case of anticipated debt liquidation, a certain small additional charge for amortization. Now, if a public improvement be self-supporting or profitable, there is no burden upon the taxpayers, and the necessity for this constitutional restriction falls. The danger to be avoided, in the judgment of your Commission, is the possibility of a public work, in its inception profitable, becoming subsequently unprofitable—and this not so much by natural causes as by legislation enacted in deference to a supposed public demand.

Take, for example, the existence of a subway municipally owned and operated—something which might be a realizable fact under such an amendment to the Constitution. Such a project might be operated profitably by the City on the basis of a five-cent fare; but if, in deference to public agitation, the Legislature should require the City to operate such a road on a three-cent fare or a two-cent fare, or for no fare at all, the "burden of debt" would instantly reassert itself and with crushing force.

While favoring the principle of the exemption of debts incurred for self-sustaining public enterprises, we emphatically condemn any further measure of relief from the salutary safeguards of the Constitution, which does not carry with it an equivalent protection for the taxpayers. No further progress along the lines of the constitutional amendment of 1905 seems either desirable or safe.

Your Commission, therefore, has deemed it the part of wisdom to prepare a conservative plan for a proposed constitutional amendment which, while exempting from the terms of the constitutional limitation bonds issued for self-supporting enterprises, would at the same time provide a nearly automatic scheme by which, should such an enterprise ever become non-supporting, the bonds issued to defray its cost would immediately be counted in estimating the City's indebtedness.

The expression of this idea in a form suitable for incorporation in the Constitution has proved to be a matter of some difficulty. In our opinion it is necessary that some tribunal should be named which should determine periodically what debts incurred by the City should not in a given time be included in determining the City's indebtedness, because of the fact that the undertakings for which they were incurred were self-supporting.

We believe that the Appellate Division of the Supreme Court is the proper tribunal, because that body has satisfactorily discharged a similar function in regard to the determination of transportation routes imposed upon it by the State Constitution.

It will be noticed that care has been taken in framing the proposed amendment, to give all persons interested, including the representatives of both the City and the State and the public generally, the right to appear before the Appellate Division and oppose or support any proposition for the exclusion of bonds in the ascertainment of the City's debt-incurring power. This suggestion has been made for two reasons: First, to insure publicity; secondly, in the hope that because of the enlightening discussion incident to the public hearings the Appellate Division would in the course of time work out a consistent theory as to net revenue above expenses much more satisfactory than any that could be outlined in advance, which was based more or less on *a priori* grounds.

In conclusion we find that the adoption of this amendment and its application by the courts would add to the margin of permissible indebtedness about one hundred and forty million dollars, representing the exclusion of bonds outstanding for the following purposes and in the following amounts:

For subways	$45,000,000 00
For docks	56,000,000 00
For water purposes prior to 1904	39,000,000 00
Total	$140,000,000 00

Following is the constitutional amendment proposed:

Amend section 10 of article 8 of the Constitution of the State of New York as the same was amended by popular vote in November, 1905, by inserting after the words:

> " except that debts incurred by the City of New York after the first day of January, nineteen hundred and four, to provide for the supply of water, shall not be so included,"

the words following:

> " and except further that debts heretofore or hereafter incurred by the said city for the acquisition of property or for the construction of railroads, docks or other improvements which shall be owned by the said city, shall not be so included if it shall appear by the ascertainment and determination hereinafter provided that the said city is receiving current net income from such property or improvement in excess of the interest payable by the said city upon the total debt incurred for the acquisition of such property or the making of such improvement. The appellate division of the supreme court in the first department shall, from time to time, upon the application of the board of estimate and apportionment or other chief financial board of the said city, ascertain and by order determine the existing

debt or debts incurred by it for such acquisition of property or the making of such improvement and which shall not be so included, provided that such ascertainment and determination shall be upon notice to the governor and attorney general of the state and to the mayor of the said city and upon other reasonable public notice to be prescribed by the court, and that the attorney general, either upon his own motion or upon the direction of the governor, and the mayor of the said city, and any resident of the said city who shall be the owner of real estate therein, duly assessed for taxation, shall be entitled to appear and to be heard in the proceeding for such ascertainment and determination, and provided further that any such ascertainment and determination shall be valid and effectual only for such period as shall be prescribed therein not exceeding five years from and after the making thereof, but shall not prevent the making of any new ascertainment and determination whether during or after such period."

Attention is called to the fact that, owing to the constitutional provision requiring amendments to be approved by two successive legislatures not having the same senate, before being submitted to vote of the people, the earliest date at which this proposed amendment could be made effective would be 1910.

Dated April 2, 1907.

Respectfully submitted,

E. J. LEVEY,
Chairman.

LAWSON PURDY,
Secretary.

ADVISORY COMMISSION

ON

TAXATION AND FINANCE

REPORT

ON

THE SYSTEM OF ACCOUNTS AND STATISTICS OF
THE CITY OF NEW YORK

JUNE, 1907

Report on the System of Accounts and Statistics of the City of New York.

Hon. George B. McClellan, *Mayor:*

Sir—Accepting as a principle, that the purpose of accounts and statistics is to obtain an intelligent basis for control over the business of the City, it follows that the nature of its accounts and statistics should be such as will make this control effective. Under the Charter of New York there are essentially two forms of control to be exercised, viz: (1) *Financial,* and (2) *Executive or Operative.*

For the purpose of exercising financial control the corporate machinery provided consists of (1) an office or division, under the direction of the Comptroller, for the exercise of accounting control, and for the issue of corporate bonds; (2) The City Treasury, the chief officer of which is the City Chamberlain; (3) Commissioners for the Selection and Approval of Depositories of the funds of the City; (4) Commissioners of the Sinking Funds; (5) the Board of Estimate and Apportionment. To the end of providing the Finance Department with the information necessary to *financial control,* there has also been installed in the City a thorough system of appropriation and fund accounts which are under the direction of its official head—the Comptroller.

With devices for exercising *executive or operative* control over its affairs, the City is not so well provided. The controlling accounts of the Department of Finance, as well as its departmental accounts, belong essentially to the first category. There has been in the City a general lack of accounting devices for obtaining accurate information by means of which the properties and liabilities and the income and expenses of the City may be intelligently administered. To this time, but little attention has been given to municipal cost keeping and to the financial and operative aspects of property administration.

Defects in the Present System of Accounts and Statistics.

More concretely the defects in the present system of accounts and statistics of the City of New York may be stated as follows:

1. Although the City is the owner of many tracts and parcels of real estate no adequate record has been kept of this property;

at the time that our committee made its examination, the City did not have a complete record as to the location, description, character of title, cost, or present condition of the real estate owned by the Corporation; there was not even a system of maps or charts which completely showed the location of such properties. Without a complete account of real estate there is no assurance to be given and only incomplete information to be had as to whether it is paying the taxes and assessments, which it should pay on its own properties. This also gives opportunity for those in subordinate administrative relation through secret contracts and other methods, to utilize city properties for political favors and for private income, as well as holds out an inducement to employees to continue other practices which, if known, would be publicly condemned.

2. There being no complete system of controlling accounts over assets, resources of the City in the form of revenues receivable were carried on collateral or memorandum records. There had not been an accounting for the arrears of taxes and assessments which constituted assets of the various municipalities consolidated with the City of New York in the year 1898. It thus appears that not only was a considerable amount of the revenues of the city in danger of being lost through neglect, but there was also a constant temptation placed in the hands of clerks to deal with those who were obligated to the City for the payment of assessments and arrears.

3. The same was true of assets in the form of stocks of material on hand and personal property with which the officers and the agents of the City were chargeable. In the several departments examined, the records of store or stock yard entries were not under direct accounting control; these records therefore might be arbitrarily brought into adjustment at periods of inventory taking, or might not be adjusted at all, without the fact being discovered except after a long and expensive examination and report.

4. The system of controlling accounts not being complete over current and contingent liabilities, many of the records showing the indebtedness of the City were essentially in the nature of memorandum accounts. Without an adequate system of central control over such records, the completeness and accuracy of accounts of indebtedness may be determined only by occasional and collateral investigation. These books or collateral records, in

many instances, have no direct relation to the general or detailed appropriation accounts under the control of the Department of Finance. As a result of this lack of records, both the city and those contracting with it, are at the mercy of uncontrolled subordinates in the Civil Service; bills presented to the several departments for approval after the delivery of goods may be withheld for months, while others, for consideration, may be forwarded out of their regular turn. Without collusion or even knowledge on his part, the Comptroller may be placed in the attitude of contributing to a wholesale levy of tribute on those who have business relations with the City.

5. The Department of Finance had no regular controlling accounting device for determining the accuracy of other departmental records showing revenues accrued to the City, whether these revenues be in the form of licenses, rates, fees, rentals of properties, or other income applicable to the expenses of a particular period. Generally speaking, the departmental records of revenues accrued were carried as collateral memoranda and not as an essential detail of general accounts. As a result uncollected water rates, rentals, etc., might go for years uncollected, or if collected, the amounts received by the officers or agents of the City might not be brought to the attention of the Comptroller through trial balances regularly taken off from subsidiary books and as supporting details to the general records kept by the Comptroller.

6. The same was true of expenses incurred by the several offices and departments, the essential accounts under control being those of appropriation and funds. Departmental expense and books of records showing departmental cost, which were kept for the information of those in positions of administrative responsibility, were not regularly proved to the books of the Comptroller. Even in the Departments themselves, control over the accuracy of expense and of stock records, where such record is kept, was incomplete.

7. There being no regular controlling accounting method of obtaining accurate data with respect to income and expenses, little effort was made to co-ordinate income and expenses within the Water Department and the Department of Docks and Ferries, which are presumably operated on a cemmercial basis, and there was no regular accounting device for bringing the general revenues of the City for a particular year into comparison with expenses of the same period, the comparative results available being

those of cash received and cash disbursed. The Mayor and other administrative officers, when desiring information with respect to the cost of any particular branch of municipal activity, are able to obtain this information only after a special examination has been made, the accuracy of the results of which may not be readily proved—an examination entailing delay that often defeats the very purpose of the inquiry. Moreover, the time of the staffs of the commissioners of accounts, and of the Bureau of Statistics of the Comptroller's office is largely occupied with special examinations to obtain information that should come currently and regularly through departmental accounts and reports, thus diverting the energies of two branches of the municipal service away from the work on which they would be more effectively employed in aid of the administration of the city's affairs.

8. The lack of controlling accounts over expenses of departments has caused the City to operate on a false basis. Many millions of dollars of the proceeds of bond issues have been used to meet the current expenses of the City which should have been included and covered into the annual tax levies for meeting current expenses, and many millions of dollars of the bonded debt of the City are represented by such expenditures for which no property or thing of value remains the proceeds having been used for current salaries and wages and for current supplies which have disappeared, without this fact coming to public attention. It is only fair to state, however, that this unfortunate result is in part due to specific statutory enactment.

9. There being no method of controlled cost keeping, independent of appropriation accounts (certain large items of departmental expenses not being charged against department appropriations) the City may not even closely approximate the cost of operating its several branches or divisions of service. For example, the cost of printing and stationery, the cost of certain items of Furniture and Fixtures, the cost of heat, light and power, the cost to the City for office space used by a department when occupying buildings belonging to the City, etc., etc., have not appeared as a part of the departmental budget receiving supplies or the benefit of such use, for the reason that these supplies or costs have been met by independent appropriations made to cover them.

10. By reason of the City having no regularly controlled accounting method of obtaining departmental expenses and by reason of the practice of making independent appropriations for such

items of expenditures as above indicated, central administrative and accounting control over such branches of the service as the City Record and the Borough Presidents' offices has been largely lost. The cost of printing and stationery being charged against appropriations to the City Record, the cost of such items as furniture and heat and light being charged against other appropriations not included in the departmental budgets where such supplies are used, not only do the departmental estimates give a false report of expenses but the accounting officers have no regular means of checking the accuracy of the accounts of divisions furnishing these supplies. That is, since the accounts and reports from departments using the materials and supplies furnished may not be used as a check on the stock accounts from which the materials were sent, regular administrative control over such branches of the municipal service as the City Record and Borough Presidents' offices are to a large extent impaired, a special and comprehensive examination being necessary to acquire the information needed as a basis for executive or other controlling judgment.

11. By a system of accounting, such as that employed by the City of New York, which charges against department appropriations the goods and supplies directly when purchased, administrative and accounting control is lost or is in a large measure impaired when such goods or material are first carried into stock. For example, in the Department of Bellevue and Allied Hospitals, in the Health Department, and in a number of other departments, most of the supplies purchased go directly to storerooms, little information being obtainable from the invoice itself as to where the supplies will be used. In Bellevue these are first delivered to a general store, then, on requisition, they are sent to the stores of the several hospitals included in the Department, from which in turn they are sent to the several wards or messes or to other branches of the services where they are finally consumed. The lack of an accurate cost accounting in many instances, opens the way to the diversion of supplies to private uses without discovery. Another result of this defect in records and reports is that those in positions of central control have no regular accounting method to accurately determine whether contractors are fairly dealing with the City through the several departments.

12. The necessity for detailed information with respect to expenses, distinct from charges against appropriations, as a guide

to administration in the departments, has given rise to the development of a large number of uncontrolled statistical records which are designed to lend themselves to departmental uses. In each of the departments concerning which definite investigation was made, the volume of work carried on is as great, in some instances far greater, than would be necessary to keep a complete system of controlled records of income and expenses with collateral operative statistics in any detail that might be desired. The effect of the lack of such controlled accounts and of the exercise of control over those departmental records is that all of the income and expense and stock records of the department are in the nature of uncontrolled statistical data. These statistical data not only suffer from inaccuracy, but have no basis or method of coordination such as would be provided if the administrative financial data required were made a part of the system of controlled accounts from the details of which regular trial balances would be made as a necessary means of supporting a general record or account.

13. Another serious defect in the present system is that the income and expenses could not be regularly audited except at an expense far greater than should be incurred in proving the accuracy of departmental records. As a result, departmental records are not at the present time regularly audited; in fact, the records of some of the departments have not been audited for years. To properly audit the departmental books of the City of New York as at present kept would make necessary the employment of a much larger staff than is at present engaged in the office of Commissioner of Accounts and in the office of Comptroller even though these offices were not encumbered with unnecessary work. With a system of complete accounting control over departmental accounts of income and expenses, as well as appropriations, it may be said that assuming an efficiency equal to that obtainable in private business the number of examiners of accounts now employed in the office of Commissioner of Accounts would be adequate. Private corporations doing a business involving as many transactions as does the business of the City of New York and having departments much more diversified, with branches and activities scattered over a Continent, some of which even have international business relations and departments, maintain not only complete and regular audits of each office and branch from one to three times a year, but also, in addition, avail themselves of annual inde-

pendent audits by public accountants at a cost far less than is at present incurred by the Municipality. On the other hand private corporations and municipalities having a much smaller volume of business when not under a centralized accounting control, over income and expenses as well as properties and liabilities, have found it impossible to make regular audits except at enormous expense; in such instances either no adequate audit has been made or the cost of examination has been so large as to compel the companies and municipalities making them to introduce a system of accounting control over departments and branch offices. It is a matter of multiplied experience that central control over income and expenses, as well as over funds and other proprietary accounts, is not only essential to careful management, but necessary to bring the cost of audit and inspection within reasonable limits; and further, that corporations, both public and private, cannot afford to be without such control.

Constructive Suggestions as to Methods of Accounting.

The accounting requirements of a municipality differ from those of an ordinary business corporation principally in this—that in addition to the information concerning Income and Expenses and Assets and Liabilities required for intelligent management, the City obtains control over its finances through a budget. Appropriation accounts are therefore necessary as a means of knowing the amount of funds available for the various purposes or for the various offices and Departments to which authority has been given to spend. In the past, it has been for this latter purpose only that the general controlling accounts of the City have been kept by the Department of Finance—income and expense, current asset and liability and property accounts having been deemed unessential or only an incident or as memoranda to the appropriation and Fund accounts. As a means of meeting the demands of the Executive, and of the people, for accurate information—as a means of enabling Department Heads to obtain the data necessary for economic and efficient administration and to the protection of municipal properties and the good faith of employees, the system of direct accounting control over the affairs of the City should be extended in such manner as to include Departmental records. This may be done by installing a uniform system of departmental accounting and by the installing in the office of Comptroller a system of controlling accounts over departmental income and expenses and over current as well as the capital assets and liabilities of the City. The detailed income and expense accounts (kept in the several departments subject to this general control) would enable them not only to report the general operative results but also regularly to lay before departmental and operative heads statements of income and expenses in such detail as is required. The following form of Summary or General Report of the Water Systems is suggested not as a final draft of recommendation, but rather to indicate the general financial and operative relations which should be reported from the departmental income and expense accounts and the general character of physical and operative statistics necessary to administrative direction and control:

GENERAL SUMMARY OF INCOME AND EXPENSES OF THE WATER SYSTEMS OF THE CITY OF NEW YORK FOR THE MONTH ENDED 190 .

	Total for the month	Total for months of the current year	Total for months of the past year	Increases or decreases
INCOME				
I. Water Rates:				
(a) Regular..................				
(b) Meter....................				
Total Water Rates..........				
I. P ermits:				
(a) Land				
(b) Marine..				
Total Permits..............				
III. Miscellaneous................				
Total Miscellaneous........				
Total of all Income from Water..................				
EXPENSES				
Administration:				
(a) General......				
(b) Borough				
Total Administration........				
II. Collection and Storage:				
(a) Operation and Maintenance.				
1. Watersheds............				
2. Aqueducts and Reservoirs...............				
3. Pumping stations.......				
4. Other................				
Total Collection and Storage.				
III. Distribution:				
(a) Operation..............				
1. Revenue Collection..				
2. Patrol and Inspection				
(b) Maintenance...........				
1. Pipe Yards.........				
2. District Repairs and Replacements				
Total Distribution.........				

	Total for the month	Total for months of the current year	Total for months of of the past year	Increases or decreases
IV. General Property Expenses, Etc.:				
(*a*) Taxes..................				
(*b*) Insurance..............				
(*c*) Interest on Bonds........				
(*d*) Depreciation				
1. Of Production and Storage Plants....				
2. Of Distributing Plants...........				
(*e*)				
(*f*)				
Total General Property Expenses, Etc...............				
Total of all Expenses for Water..................				
Excess of Income over Expenses....				
Excess of Expenses over Income....				
Cash Receipts:				
1. Collections on account of Previous Period................				
(*a*) Water Rates:				
(1) Regular............				
(2) Meter..............				
(3)				
(*b*) Permits:				
(1) Land				
(2) Marine.............				
(*c*) Miscellaneous				
2. Collections on account of Current Period..................				
(*a*) Water Rates:				
(1) Regular............				
(2) Meter..............				
(3)				
(*b*) Permits:				
(1) Land				
(2) Marine				
(*c*) Miscellaneous.........				
Total Cash Collections......				
Excess of Cash Collections over Income Accrued..................				
Excess of Income Accrued over Cash Collections....................				

	Total for the month	Total for months of the current year	Total for months of the past year	Increases or decreases
Uncollected Accounts Receivable:				
1. At Beginning of Period.......				
(a) More than 1 month and less than 3 overdue...				
(b) More than 3 months and and less than 1 year overdue				
2. Accrued during Period				
Total.....................				
3. Collected during Period.......				
4. Balance at end of Period......				
Liability for Accounts Paid in Advance				
Excess of Accounts Received over Liability for Accounts Paid in Advance				
Cost of Plants:				
1. Cost of Plants less Depreciation and Losses at beginning of Period.....................				
2. Cost of Construction during Period				
(a) Supervision and Inspection.................				
1. Of Extensions........				
2. Of High Pressure systems				
(b) Outlays for Plants during Period				
(1) For Extensions......				
(1) For High Pressure...				
3. Depreciation and Losses during Period.....................				
4. Cost of Plants Less Depreciation at the end of the Period.....				
Operative Statistics:				
Number Gallons Received in City Reservoirs..................				
Number Gallons Discharged from City Reservoirs...............				
Wastage at Reservoirs (Gal.).....				
" " " (Per ct.)...				

	Total for the month	Total for months of the current year	Total for months of the past year	Increases or decreases
Number Gallons delivered:				
Regular Service................				
Meter Service..................				
Wastage from Mains, Pipes (Gal.)				
Wastage from M. P. (Per ct.)...				
Cost of Production per 1,000 Gallons Produced				
Cost of Distribution per 1,000 Gallons Delivered				
Total Cost of 1,000 Gallons Delivered				
Percentage of Total Cost:				
For Administration				
For Distribution..............				
For General Property Expenses, Etc.....................				
Average Meter Rates per 1,000 Gallons				
Average Regular Rates per 1,000 Gallons				

While the Commission has gone to considerable length into this and other Departments, the exact details are not for us to recommend. These should be worked out in conference with the Comptroller and the several parties in interest, after an exhaustive study of every phase of each branch of activity. If, upon such inquiry, it should be found that any of the items suggested should be changed to better adapt a form to administration and accounting use, such alterations or changes may be made without impairing the principle of publicity suggested.

For the information of the several heads of the Water Systems, as well as for the information of the Head of the Department, the Income and Expense, as well as the collateral physical and operative statistics of each separately operated systems, should be regularly reported in detail from the accounts and subsidiary records. Assuming that the detailed account, as well as the detailed reports of the several Boroughs or systems may have a common classification, the detailed reports from the Borough accounting offices where the Income and Expense Ledgers are kept may be used as journal entries for the accounts of the central office of the Department, thus enabling the Chief Bookkeeper of the Departments to render a report in detail, for each of the systems, or a consolidated report for them all in a form desired within a few days after the closing of each calendar month. For example: The expenses of each administrative office may be classified to show (1) Salaries and Wages; (2) Office Expense; (3) Miscellaneous Administrative Expenses with details under each classification something as follows:

(1) Salaries and Wages
- Commissioner, Superintendent or Head
- Assistants
- Clerks
- Stenographers
- ....
- ....

(2) Office Expenses
- Rent
- Heat and Light
- Printing and Stationery
- Postage
- Office Furniture and Fittings
- Telephone, Telegraph and Commercial Messenger
- ....
- ....

(3) Miscellaneous Expenses
- Transportation
- Carriage and Horse Hire
- Automobile Expenses
- ....
- ....

A common classification may also be established for laboratories, pumping stations, filtering plants and each of the operative divisions of the several systems, thus supplying for each system a common basis for reporting in detail items of expense and which may finally be grouped and summarized in a general report. Upon such classification, detailed expense accounts may be established in each of the Borough Offices over which an accounting control may be exercised by the central accounting office of the Department, and which in turn may be controlled from the offices of Mayor and Comptroller. By the installation of properly classified expense accounts in each of the departments, and general expense accounts over each of the departments in the office of Comptroller, a complete expense accounting may be made effective and information will come regularly to those in administrative relation necessary to judgment in the direction and control of the City's business.

The Advantages of Accounts which Show Expenses as Distinct and Separate from Appropriations.

Objection has been raised to the keeping of expense accounts as distinct from and independent of appropriation accounts. Those who have criticised the introduction of this class of accounts affirm that there is no need for distinct accounts to show expenses. As opposed to this view, however, it is to be noted that in a system containing budgetary accounts only, no place is found for any item of expense which does not represent a charge against an appropriation. In such a system no place may be found for such classes of expenses, as printing and stationery, heat and light, furniture and fixtures obtained from other departments, for an apportionment of salaries and wages, depreciation, etc., etc. Printing and stationery being furnished to the several departments by the City Record, the purchases of stationery supplies must be entered against appropriations for the support of the City Record, and although a register may be kept which contains information as to requisitions for printing and stationery made by a Department, there is no provision in the controlled departmental accounts for exercising direct supervision and audit over this class of expenses incurred. The same is true of office furniture and fittings which are purchased by the Borough Presidents and of the cost of providing the Department with office space, etc. Neither is there any provision made for the proper accounting for the use of a large part of the supplies which are purchased by the Departments themselves and taken into stock before being distributed. These are charged to Appropriations of the Department when purchased. When operating on a basis of appropriation accounting only, the fact that no accounting device may be introduced which will indicate the disposition of these supplies to the various branches of the Department where used over which control may be exercised, suggests one of the many reasons why the Department should have *expense accounts* that are independent and distinct from *appropriation accounts.*

A department of Municipal activity should have an accounting means of determining the cost of operation as accurately and as promptly as would be if its authority to spend did not come through appropriations. The expense incurred by a Department for supplies is not reflected by the amount purchased and taken into stock. For example: The Water Department of the City of New York might purchase many thousands of dollars' worth of pipe, materials and plumbing supplies during any month of the year, while only a small portion of this stock may be used during the period reported on. From an operative point of view the officers and the public wish to know what is the relation of the cost of operation to the Income or other provision made for meeting the cost and whether the several systems of Water Supply are being economically managed. When construction and repairs are the objects of expenditure, as well as in cases of the consumption of consumable goods, the labor and materials actually used is the only basis for judgment as to economy. To throw into the expense accounts purchases for stock, destroys all comparisons and subverts judgment, both with respect to operative results and with respect to efficiency and economy of service. In determining questions of expense, account should be taken of the wear and waste to the plant even though no provision be made for repairs and replacements. The introduction of distinct accounts which will reflect expenses as separate and apart from the provision made for the payment of claims against the City on account of purchases, would accomplish this result. Without such accounts this information would not be available.

Administrative Advantage of Accounts and Reports of Properties and Capital Outlays.

Under a system which makes provision for budgetary accounts only, there are no centrally controlled accounts showing the operations, the cost, and present condition of properties. This is true for the same reason that there are no accounts giving true expenses. When an expenditure is made, it is written against an appropriation. The result is to show the balance of appropriations unexpended and in the contra-entry may be shown the total or aggregate of appropriations for a specified purpose. These accounts are proper and necessary to financial control, but they give little or no true information with respect to operating results or proprietary condition. For purposes of illustration, let us assume that there are certain Department properties to be administered in the form of office buildings. That we may know whether the buildings are economically managed and kept in regular repair, an account and report should be made on each property to show some such relations as the following:

SUMMARY OF EXPENSES OF REAL ESTATE

	Total of All Buildings	Description of Properties	
		City Hall	Hall of Records
General Administration :			
Salaries—Wages....................			
Clerks, etc........................			
Superintendents.			
Office Expenses....................			
Total Cost of Administration...			
Operation :			
Salaries—Wages.....			
Elevator Men.......			
Engineers, Oilers and Helpers.....			
Electrician			
Janitors, Porters, Cleaners, etc....			
Special Officers and Watchmen....			
Other Wages—Operations.........			
Supplies..........................			
Fuel, Oil and Waste...............			
Electrical Supplies			
Janitors' Supplies			
Heat, and Light Purchased			
Other Supplies—Operations.......			
Total Cost of Operations........			
Maintenance :			
Repairs and Replacements			
Buildings and Grounds............			
Elevators.........................			
Engines and Boilers, etc..........			
Electrical Machinery......... ...			
Other Repairs and Replacements ..			
Depreciation.....................			
Total Cost of Maintenance......			
General Property Expenses :			
Taxes			
Insurance........................			
Ground Rents			
Other Property Expenses..........			
Total General Property Expenses			
Total Expenses......................			

A proper classification of accounts needed for reporting on the proprietary relations of buildings of the character above indicated might be:

	Cost.	Depreciation.
Sites and Grounds..................		
Buildings Structures		
Elevators		
Power & Heating Plants............		
Electrical Equipment		
Fittings & Fixtures.................		

The object of any classification of property accounts adopted is: to show, with respect to each building, the character and original cost of improvements, additions and betterments; to enable the Board of Estimate and Apportionment, as well as the operative heads, to make provision for maintenance based on engineering experience; and to determine whether the provisions for repairs and replacements are adequate or if not the measure of depreciation or inadequacy of provision for wear and waste—that is the amount of expenditures that had been deferred during a current period for which provision must be made in subsequent budgets. As a means of determining whether the buildings have been adequately maintained, there may be set up a reserve for depreciation (based on engineering experience) which reserve would be regularly charged to expenses. When repairs are made the reserves may be debited and the audited vouchers for stock accounts credited with such an accounting, the credit balance of the reserve account will show the amount of the depreciation; a debit balance would be in the nature of prepaid expenses or betterments.

As a means of obtaining a true account and report on the operations of the buildings, it would be necessary to have both property and expense accounts—the same property and expense accounts as if no consideration were to be given to the method or means of obtaining funds. A clear line of distinction, therefore, should be drawn between the supplies and materials used and supplies and materials in stock; between repairs and replacements actually made and depreciation; between additions and betterments to property and expenses of operation and maintenance; between the taxes, insurance and rents of other expense charges to the current period and the expenditure of amounts for periods past or future, although the payment for taxes, insurance, rents, etc., were made during the current period and were chargeable against current appropriations. Such relations may be currently and accurately shown only by having the property accounts and expense accounts and by keeping these accounts entirely distinct from the appropriation accounts. The budgetary accounts and the property and expense accounts are essentially different in purpose and one class or character of accounts may not be successfully used for the purpose of giving the data intended to be shown through the other.

Administrative Advantage of Operative Statistics.

When Income and Expense accounts distinct from Appropriation accounts are kept, all of the operative financial results are brought under direct accounting control and may be obtained from the regular footings and balances shown on the books. The physical and operative statistics which may not be stated in terms of dollars and cents, however, are not and may not be regularly retained through the accounts. These statistics must be kept in separate statistical records and should be so co-ordinated with the accounts that each may be used to supplement the other in giving the information needed for determining any factor or result of management required.

Detailed Suggestions as to Accounting and Reporting.

We have not attempted in this report to do more than suggest general principles of accounting and reporting, which may be applied to the financial as well as the operative management of a City, believing that if the principles herein suggested be approved by the City Administration further investigation should be undertaken with a view of receiving a detailed plan of accounting control for permanent adoption.

Difficulties to be Encountered in the Revision of the Present System.

While under the law the Comptroller of the City of New York is authorized to introduce and enforce upon the departments any form of accounting which he may direct, the difficulties to be encountered by him in any effort which he may make to reorganize the accounts of the City should not be passed without notice. In the first place the departmental accounts of the City of Greater New York are, in a large measure, made up of those which have been taken over from a number of dissimilar municipalities and brought together by consolidation. Each of these municipalities has had its own administrative methods and departmental practices. Moreover, the corporation of Greater New York is dependent for the details of administration on a clerical staff which is not subject to direct control by the central officers of the City. The present method of appointment and removal of the clerical staff not only deprives the Comptroller of powers to enforce, but even the heads of the departments themselves have in numerous instances found themselves unable through discipline or otherwise to establish a policy of sufficient independence to enable them to direct and accomplish results which have been deemed essential to economic and efficient management.

Another fact to be recognized is that the Comptroller is essentially a political and financial officer. He is elected to a position of responsibility with little or no knowledge of the business over which he is to exercise controlling judgment and with accounting methods in vogue that do not provide the information needed in the performance of his duties. Being the chief financial officer of the City, little of his time or attention may be given to matters of accounting or to the reorganization of the system. As an officer he finds himself in a position of legal responsibility for the acts and methods of hundreds of officials and non-official subordinates, who, in groups and departments, are transacting the business of the City along lines of inherited custom. Not having the appointment of the accounting heads of other departments, within his control, and the members of the staff not being directly subject to discipline, the institution as it has developed moves with a momentum and possesses an inertia so great at times to annul his authority. To organize the accounts on a new basis, to successfully devise, install and supervise a system of control over income and expenses, as well as over appropriation and proprietary accounts, would require the undivided attention and unlimited power of a Comptroller through his entire period of incumbency. Being engrossed in the financial affairs of his office, he must necessarily depend upon the advice of others.

Recommendation With Respect to the Offices of Comptroller and Commissioners of Accounts.

In our opinion, a change both in accounting methods and in organization is necessary to effective administrative control. In effecting such change two distinct lines of development are possible:

(1) The hands of the Comptroller may be further strengthened, by not only permitting him, when it may be considered desirable, to call to his assistance independent professional advice in devising and installing improved methods, but also by giving him a freer hand in the removal of departmental accounting heads and chief assistants, when, in his judgment, such heads or assistants may prove inefficient, thus enabling him to impress upon the several departments of the City such reform as may be properly approved for the purpose of instituting a more rigid control and of efficiently administering a thorough system of executive and operative accounts. The advantage of the plan above suggested would be that accounting control would be centralized and there might be the greatest economy and uniformity in the administration of the system.

Complementary to such a disposition of accounting control there should also be a change made in the scope and purpose of the office of Commissioners of Accounts. Although in the past this office has been used principally as a statistical bureau and incidentally as an auditing bureau, as a complement to a system of controlled accounts it has in it the possibility of becoming one of the most important divisions of city government. Instead of encumbering the staff of this office with the making of perfunctory reports on questions of current administration the information with respect to which should come regularly from the departments, the office of Commissioners should be principally occupied (*a*) with auditing the accounts and reports of departments, and (*b*) as a court of expert inquiry for the information of the Mayor with respect to administration, *i. e.,* as an inquisitorial branch of the executive for the determination of facts that could not ordinarily be reached by an auditor without such powers as are possessed by the Commissioners of Accounts while sitting as a special court with authority to subpœna witnesses, and to require the production of books and other evidence necessary to the determination of facts not found on the face of the records. Being provided with an adequate system of departmental accounts under the Comptroller and being thus armed with an independent bureau of departmental audit under the Commissioner of Accounts, with all of the powers of the Legislature to inquire into every transaction in which the city may be interested, there is no reason why the Mayor may not fully perform the duties imposed by the charter, viz.: "to keep himself informed of the doings of "the several departments;" "to be vigilant and active in causing the ordinances of the City and laws of the State to be executed and enforced;" "and generally to perform all such duties "as may be prescribed for him."

(2) A second suggestion involves a somewhat more radical change in Charter provisions. The Comptroller is to-day much encumbered with political and legislative duties. Originally, when New York was a City less than one-fifth its present size, the Comptroller was little more than the City's chief bookkeeper and auditing officer. To-day, he is the chief officer of financial control. As a member of the Board of Estimate and Apportionment, Sinking Fund Commission, etc., and as a member *ex-officio* of other boards, these functions together with his other duties—largely legislative—have tended to overshadow his original accounting functions. Vested, by statute, with power to dictate the form of accounting in other departments, in practice, for many years past the Comptroller has found little or no time to give such matters his attention, and the heterogeneous and incongruous methods of accounting inherited from the past have gone on unaltered. On the other hand, the Mayor, charged by law with the duty of keeping himself advised as to all matters of administration, has been helpless to an astonishing degree. The Commissioners of Accounts, who should have been the means of enlightening him, through digests of monthly and annual reports made by the departments, have, as already stated, been largely occupied with the making of special examination which have taken much time and labor and which would have been unnecessary under a proper system of accounting control. They have, it is true, furnished him with such information as he received, but this has been fragmentary and so far in arrears of the transactions reported on as to make them of little value for administrative purposes.

In 1906 the Legislature established in the Comptroller's Office, a Bureau of Statistics—another blind striving to obtain facts through special investigation which should come regularly from departmental accounts in the form of well digested monthly and annual reports. The City is in the attitude of having two bureaus for the assembling and reporting of statistics without having the regular accounting machinery for supplying currently the information necessary for making such bureaus effective.

For the purpose of maintaining effective financial control, all bills and claims against the City should, as now, be approved by the Comptroller; he should remain in control of the City's budgetary and financial accounts, and he should be left free to pursue those most important legislative duties which have been imposed upon him. To this end the office of Comptroller may be entirely relieved from all responsibility for the administrative accounts, *i. e.,* control over the department records essential to executive efficiency and administrative economy may be transferred to the office of Commissioners of Accounts. As the Mayor is made responsible for administrative results, so he may then have in his hands, the means of acquiring knowledge of administrative defects and, through his power of removal, may then enforce remedies as faults are made known. Were this second principle adopted as the theory of reorganization of the accounting methods, the Commissioners of Accounts should then be vested with the power to devise and install bookkeeping methods and systems in all departments of the City Government, excepting in the office of the Comptroller and should be given power to remove departmental accounting heads.

Another advantage of having the accounts and statistics which look toward executive or operative control (as distinguished from fund and appropriation accounts) devised, installed and supervised by the Commissioners of Accounts, would be that the Commissioners are appointed by and responsible to the Mayor. The Comptroller is by law the principal officer of *financial* control and his administrative responsibilities under the Charter have been mainly of this character. As such officer, it has been incumbent on him to devise and install a system of controlling financial accounting; but having no responsibility for the *economy* or *efficiency* of departments, and being independent of the Mayor, there has been no provision in the Charter making it his duty to devise, install or control executive and operative accounts. The interests of the Comptroller having been centered in *financial* control, "the forms for keeping and rendering the accounts," have been principally for his information only. As a result, the Mayor as Chairman of the Board of Estimate and Apportionment, has been subordinate in elicited intelligence to the Comptroller; as the chief executive of Departments, he has been dependent for current information on one who has no official interest in, or responsibility for, departmental results; he has been compelled to administer his office with no adequate method for assembling *operative* administrative data.

In any case, it is our opinion that the Charter should be so amended as to render accounting control consistent with efficient administration. In other words, given an adequate system of accounts, the Mayor would seem to have ample power to protect the interests of the City. Being constituted by law "a magistrate," as well as "the chief executive officer of the city," and having at will the power to appoint and remove Commissioners of Accounts who have the fullest authority, not only to audit departmental accounts, but also to sit as a court of inquiry, there would seem to be in the hands of the Mayor the means not only of protecting the City against spoilation through contracts, but also to establish the incompetency or infidelity of those in the Civil Service who in the past have enjoyed immunity from discipline.

ADVISORY COMMISSION

ON

TAXATION AND FINANCE

REPORT

OF

COMMITTEE ON TAXATION AND REVENUE

ON

COLLECTION OF ARREARS OF REAL ESTATE TAXES AND ASSESSMENTS

DECEMBER, 1907

The Collection of Arrears of Real Estate Taxes and Assessments.

INTRODUCTION.

Long experience in the Finance Department convinced Mr. Joseph Haag, when Chief Bookkeeper, that the method for the collection of arrears of taxes and assessments was hopelessly inadequate. In 1902 he presented to the Comptroller an outline of what he regarded as a satisfactory method. No steps were taken to work out this plain detail until a year and a half ago, when Mr. Haag presented the plan to Mr. Purdy, Chairman of the Committee on Taxation and Revenue of the Mayor's Advisory Commission. Mr. Purdy then prepared a rough draft of a bill amending Title 5 of Chapter XVII. of the Charter, which was printed and submitted to the Committee on Taxation and Revenue. The plan was so far approved by the Committee in principle that it seemed desirable to perfect the bill. The bill as prepared by Mr. Purdy was submitted to Mr. Walter Lindner, Solicitor of the Title Guarantee and Trust Company, and he became so much interested in the plan that he was kind enough to volunteer to aid the Committee. Mr. Lindner has now carefully revised the bill, inserting the provisions necessary to make it thoroughly workable, having in view the necessity for such perfection of detail as will result in the City being able to insure a perfectly good title to the purchaser of real property when ultimately sold for taxes.

Mr. Lindner has had in mind also the necessity for making the tax liens provided for in the bill an attractive investment. The Committee has also had the benefit of the advice and assistance of Mr. Edward L. Heydecker, the Editor of the General Laws of New York, now a member of the Committee.

THE PRESENT METHOD.

The present method of enforcing the payment of arrears of real estate taxes, assessments and water rents is contained in Title 5 of Chapter XVII. of the Charter and was taken, almost without change, from the Charter of the old City of New York, called The Consolidation Act. The plan in substantially its present form, has been in force for many years. Briefly described it is as follows:

Taxes, assessments and water rents are liens upon the land assessed and are preferred in payment to all other charges. When taxes or assessments are unpaid for three years and water rents for four years it is lawful for the Collector of Assessments and Arrears, under the direction of the Comptroller, to advertise for sale a lease of the property for the lowest term of years at which any person shall offer to take the same in consideration of advancing the arrears, with interest at the rate of seven per cent., to the time of sale. The purchaser of such leases receives a certificate of sale describing the property, the term of the lease, the amount of arrears, interest, etc., advanced in payment for the lease and the time when the purchaser will be entitled to the lease of the property. If there are no bids for a lease of any property offered for sale, the City of New York may bid it in for the City.

If no one interested in the property pays the amount mentioned in the certificate of sale within two years from the date of the certificate, with interest at the rate of fourteen per cent., the Comptroller shall execute to the purchaser a lease of the property for the term of years for which it has been sold. The lease cannot be executed and delivered until six months after due publication of a notice that unless the property be redeemed by a certain day, the lease will be conveyed to the purchaser.

Objections to the Sale of Leases.

The experience of the old City of New York with this method of enforcing payment of arrears has been that a very small percentage of the property put up for sale has been bid for by individuals, the bulk of the property being bid in by the representatives of the City, and the amount realized from actual sales is inconsiderable. As the sole object of the sale is to realize the amount due the City, the whole object of the plan is defeated.

Because of the small number of bidders, the leases are very long and the risk to the owners of property correspondingly great if the lease should be upheld. Leases are sold for one thousand years. This is equivalent to the sale of the fee. Under such circumstances, the owner of the property would receive nothing, his property would be totally lost because he had failed or neglected to pay the City within the time required by law a small percentage of its value. In view of this great danger to owners of property the Courts have been exceedingly vigilant to detect flaws in the procedure so that it is commonly believed that a valid lease sold for arrears is almost unknown. With the value of the leases so utterly discredited, it is no wonder there are few bidders and that when leases are sold the term of years is abnormally long.

So poor has been the result of these sales of leases that there have been only six such sales in the last thirty-two years. The objections may be summarized as follows: The expense and the danger to property owners is excessive and unreasonable. The City is unable by the sale of leases to collect its revenue when it requires it.

Some persons have suggested that the City of New York should adopt the remedy existing in the former City of Brooklyn by the sale at auction of the fee of the property. Although this method was effective in enforcing the payment of arrears, it is objectionable because too severe on property owners whose property may be sacrificed and because it is difficult to convey good title by a sale for taxes. Titles are often clouded and purchasers being obliged to take the risk of a bad title do not bid the full value of the property.

The following plan, it is deemed, would be effective in collecting arrears promptly and at the same time would impose no unconscionable penalties on property owners and in many cases would, in fact, reduce the amount of interest they may now be required to pay.

The Remedy.

To be satisfactory any method of collecting arrears of real estate taxes, assessments and water rents must combine two qualities:

The remedy must be effective and enable the City to collect arrears promptly.

The remedy must cause property owners the least possible inconvenience and risk.

The proposed remedy is deemed to meet these conditions. It is briefly described as follows:

As soon as taxes, assessments and water rents are laid, a lien attaches to the property in favor of the City, which is prior to any and all other liens. When taxes or assessments are three years in arrears, or water rents four years, the lien of all arrears which shall have accrued up to the day of the first advertisement of sale, will be sold at auction to the person who shall bid the lowest rate of interest not exceeding twelve per cent. Upon payment of the purchase money a conveyance of the "tax lien," payable in three years, will be executed by the City to the purchaser.

The City will guarantee the validity of the lien so that the only risk taken by the purchaser will be the sufficient value of the property affected by the lien and the possible trouble of collection.

"Transfers of tax liens" will be registered in the office of the Collector of Assessments and Arrears and will be recordable in the office of the Register. The procedure for collection will be the same as for the collection of a mortgage.

A "transfer of tax lien" will provide that the whole of the principal sum which the "transfer of tax lien" is given to secure shall become due at the option of the owner thereof after default in the payment of interest for thirty days or after default in the payment of any subsequently accruing tax, assessment or water rent for six months. This provision will very nearly insure the continuous future payment of taxes and assessments, subsequent to the sale of a "tax lien," as the owner of the property must pay or suffer the foreclosure of the "tax lien."

Any person having an interest in property affected by a "tax lien" may discharge the same before maturity on giving thirty days' notice to the holder of the transfer thereof upon payment of the principal with interest to a date three months subsequent to the date of payment named in the notice.

"Tax liens" will be exempt from taxation and will be made legal investments for Savings Banks in case they do not exceed half the assessed value of the property affected.

Advantages.

"Tax liens" will be a thoroughly safe investment, being absolutely the first liens on city real estate. "Tax liens" for large sums should sell readily at a low rate of interest and even "tax liens" for small sums should be a profitable investment and sell easily at some rate less than the maximum. It is probable that some persons and corporations will undertake the purchase of "tax liens" as a business, perhaps issuing debenture bonds thereby secured.

If "tax liens" are readily salable the City will no longer be kept out of the use of its proper income. The trouble and expense of collection will be shifted from the City to private parties.

As the proceedings for foreclosure will be judicial full justice will be done to delinquent owners and the courts will be careful to sustain the validity of their own acts.

From the standpoint of the taxpayer, the proposed plan has the great advantage that, when a tax is over three years in arrears all taxes and assessments then due can be postponed for three years more upon payment of interest and subsequent taxes. Moreover, the taxpayer, if a resident, will always get personal notice, and will generally get personal notice even if a non-resident, when any action is brought which might result in the sale of the property.

Description of the Bill.

The Bill amends Chapter XVII. of the New York Charter.

Section 1 of the Bill amends the caption of Chapter XVII., by inserting the words, " tax liens on " so that Title 5 shall read: " Sales of tax liens on lands for taxes, assessments and water rents."

Section 2 of the Bill amends Charter Section 909, changing the definition of water rents, by making it more specific.

Section 3 amends Charter Section 920, as amended by Chapter 303 of the Laws of 1907, by inserting the words " the tax lien."

Section 4 amends Charter Section 964 by inserting the words " the tax lien."

Section 5 of the Bill amends the caption of Title 5 so as to conform to the caption of the Chapter.

Section 6 amends Charter Section 1017 by more carefully defining " water rents." This section determines the time when taxes, assessments and water rents become liens.

Charter Sections 1018 and 1019 remain unchanged. They relate to the publication of notice of the confirmation of assessments, and the charging of interest, if assessments are unpaid after sixty days.

Section 7. Charter Section 1020 provides the rate of interest to be charged on all arrears of taxes and assessments. The section is amended to conform to the sale of the tax lien instead of a lease.

SECTION 8 amends Charter Section 1021, by providing for sale of the tax lien for arrears of assessments, and provides for apportionment by the Board of Assessors when parcels are divided.

SECTIONS 9 and 10 make slight verbal changes in Charter Sections 1023 and 1024, otherwise 1022, 1023, 1023a and 1024 remain unchanged. They relate to water rents; the return of arrears to the Collector by the Receiver of Taxes; notifying taxpayers of assessments and provision for the inclusion of water rents in the assessment rolls.

SECTION 11 amends Charter Section 1025. This section provides for the record of arrears on the assessment rolls and remains substantially unchanged.

SECTION 12 amends Charter Section 1026. This section provides for notices of arrears to be printed on tax bills and is amended to conform to the new remedy, so that warning of the sale of a "tax lien" shall be given instead of notice of the sale of the lease.

SECTION 13 amends Charter Section 1027. This section now provides the procedure for the sale of leases and is amended so as to provide for the sale of "tax liens." Such procedure is substantially unchanged. It provides that when taxes or assessments are unpaid for three years or water rents for four years, the Collector of Assessments and Arrears shall advertise "tax liens" for sale for a term of three years to the person who bids the lowest rate of interest, not exceeding twelve per cent. The Collector shall give to the purchaser of "tax liens" a "transfer of tax lien," describing the property encumbered by the lien; the sum to be paid; the amount advanced and the rate of interest. All the provisions for advertising such sales are preserved unchanged.

SECTION 14. Charter Section 1028 is repealed. It provided for the advertisement of contiguous lots as one parcel, which would endanger the accuracy of the procedure.

SECTION 15. Charter Section 1029 is renumbered so as to be 1028, and is unchanged in substance. It provides that the Comptroller may postpone sales.

SECTION 16. Charter Section 1030 is renumbered so as to be Section 1029. It provides that the Collector of Assessments and Arrears shall conduct the sales and is amended so as to provide for a deposit or payment on account by the purchaser at the time of sale upon terms and conditions prescribed by the Comptroller. "Transfers of Tax liens" shall be delivered to the purchaser, without charge, upon payment of the amount due. "Transfers of Tax liens" not paid for within thirty days may be canceled and the deposit forfeited, and a resale made.

SECTION 17. Charter Sections 1031 to 1049, both inclusive, are repealed. All these Sections relate solely to the procedure to be followed in case of the sale of leases and have no bearing upon the sale of "tax liens."

SECTION 18 enacts a new section to be numbered 1030, defining "transfer of tax lien" and describing its nature and incidents. "Transfers of Tax liens" shall be executed by or in behalf of the Collector of Assessments and Arrears.

SECTION 19 enacts a new section to be numbered 1031. It provides for a public record of sales of "Tax liens" to be kept by the Collector of Assessments and Arrears. A "transfer of tax lien" and a duly acknowledged assignment thereof shall be deemed conveyances under the Real Property Law and may be recorded as such. Failure to record does not invalidate the lien. The various records may be read in evidence.

SECTION 20 enacts a new section to be numbered 1032. This section defines the rights of purchasers of tax liens.

SECTION 21 enacts a new section to be numbered 1033, providing for the discharge of the tax lien when paid.

SECTION 22 enacts a new section to be numbered 1034, providing for the exemption from taxation of tax liens.

SECTIONS 23, 24, 25, 26, 27, 28 and 29 enact new sections to be numbered 1035, 1036, 1037, 1038, 1039, 1040 and 1041, providing the procedure for foreclosure of tax liens.

SECTION 30 adds a new section to be Section 1042. It provides for the procedure when no bid for a "tax lien" is received. In this case the Comptroller and Corporation Counsel shall investigate the facts and reduce the amount to a sum for which, in their judgment, a "tax lien" bearing twelve per cent. interest can be sold. They shall file a certificate in writing setting forth the amount so determined, with their reasons. Such "tax lien" shall then be advertised for sale to the person who shall bid the highest amount of money in excess of the amount fixed by the Comptroller and Corporation Counsel. If still no bid is received, the

Comptroller and Corporation Counsel shall reconsider their determination and proceed as before. This section is added in order that some collection may be made by the City and title cleared in cases where the arrears equal or exceed the value of the property.

SECTIONS 31 and 32 enact new sections to be numbered 1043 and 1044, providing for the reimbursement of the owner of a "transfer of tax lien" in case the tax lien shall be vacated or cancelled in whole or in part.

SECTION 33 enacts a new section to be numbered 1045. It provides that owners of property may question the validity of tax liens on their property; that such shall be referred to the Corporation Counsel, who may direct the surrender of a transfer of tax lien and the refunding of the amount paid therefor.

SECTION 34 enacts a new section to be numbered 1046. It provides that the Corporation Counsel shall be notified of any proceeding adverse to the validity of a tax lien and may intervene in such proceeding.

SECTION 35 enacts a new section to be numbered 1047. It provides for reimbursement of the holder of a transfer of lien which is invalid in whole or in part, and directs the resale of so much of the tax lien as remains valid.

SECTION 36. Charter Section 1050 is renumbered so as to be Section 1048. It provides for the delivery of a duplicate in case the "transfer of tax lien" is lost, and is otherwise without change of substance, except that the provision for registration is omitted here and inserted in Section 1031.

SECTION 37. Charter Section 1051 is renumbered so as to be 1049. It provides that bills for the arrears of taxes and assessments shall be furnished when requested. It also provides that the certificate of the Collector, countersigned by the Comptroller, shall free the property from all liens except the lien of "transfers of tax liens" duly sold. The section is unchanged except in so far as was necessary to conform the procedure to the method of collection by the sale of "tax liens" instead of leases.

SECTION 38. Charter Section 1052 is renumbered so as to be 1050. It provides that fees for searches shall be included in the bills mentioned in the preceding section and is unchanged.

SECTION 39 repeals Charter Section 1053. It provided for a complete record of sales, now contained in Section 1031.

SECTION 40. Charter Section 1054 is renumbered so as to be Section 1051. It provides for the preservation of affidavits of the publication of notices and remains unchanged.

SECTION 41. This section is not a part of the Charter and is designed to save to the city and the taxpayers all rights acquired before the passage of the Act.

The proposed bill is as follows:

AN ACT to amend the Greater New York Charter relative to sales of lands for taxes, assessments and water rates.

The People of the State of New York, represented in Senate and Assembly, do enact as follows:

SECTION 1. The caption of Chapter XVII. of the Greater New York Charter, as re-enacted by chapter four hundred and sixty-six of the laws of nineteen hundred and one, is hereby amended so as to read as follows:

CHAPTER XVII.

TAXES AND ASSESSMENTS.

Title 1. Department of Taxes and Assessments; powers and duties.

Title 2. Assessments for local improvements other than those confirmed by a Court of Record.

Title 3. Vacating and modifying assessments for local improvements other than those confirmed by a Court of Record.

Title 4. Opening Streets and Parks.

Title 5. Sales of *tax liens on* lands for taxes, assessments and water rates.

SEC. 2. Section nine hundred and nine of the Greater New York Charter, as re-enacted by chapter four hundred and sixty-six of the laws of nineteen hundred and one, is hereby amended so as to read as follows:

ASSESSMENT-ROLLS TO REMAIN IN CUSTODY OF BOARD OF ALDERMEN.

SEC. 909. The tax or assessment rolls, when finally submitted to the board of aldermen on the first Monday of July in each year, shall remain in its custody, but the president of the board may, by written permission, permit access to them, and he is hereby, in the name of the board of aldermen and as its act, authorized and directed to cause to be properly estimated and computed the taxes annually imposed, and cause the same to be properly set down or extended in the several assessment rolls or tax books, as required by the next section. It shall also be the duty of said president to cause the items of said taxes to be carefully added, and to set down the amount of the same therein; and when completed to deliver the tax books relating to real estate to the comptroller, in order that the unpaid water rents, *and the expenses of meters, with their connections and setting, water rates and other lawful charges for the supply of water measured by meters of any* **[**each**]** preceding year may be entered therein. After such completion of the assessment rolls or tax books it shall be the duty of the city clerk to procure the proper warrants authorizing and requiring the receiver of taxes to collect the several sums therein mentioned according to law, and such warrants need be signed only by the president of the board of aldermen, and countersigned by the city clerk, and immediately thereafter the president of the board of aldermen shall deliver the said assessment rolls, with the warrants aforesaid annexed thereto, to the receiver of taxes, at the same time notifying the comptroller of the amount of taxes in each book, in order that he may cause the proper sum to be charged to the receiver for collection.

SEC. 3. Section nine hundred and twenty of said law, as amended by chapter three hundred and three of the laws of nineteen hundred and seven, is hereby amended so as to read as follows:

UNDIVIDED PARTS OF TAXES: PAYMENT OF.

SEC. 920. If a sum of money in gross has been or shall be taxed upon any lands or premises, any person or persons claiming any divided or undivided part thereof may pay such part of the sum of money so taxed, also of the interest and charges due or charged thereon, as the said comptroller may deem to be just and equitable. The department of taxes and assessments shall apportion the assessed valuation of such land or premises when requested by the comptroller so to do, and shall certify such apportionment to him. The determination of the said comptroller shall be based upon such apportionment so certified. The remainder of the sum of money so taxed, together with the interest and charges, shall be a lien upon the residue of the land and premises only, *and the tax lien upon such* [which] residue may be sold to satisfy [the residue of] such tax, interest or charges *thereon,* in the same manner as though the residue of said tax had been imposed *only* upon [the] *such* residue of said lands or premises.

SEC. 4. Section nine hundred and sixty-four of said law is hereby amended so as to read as follows:

RE-ASSESSMENT.

SEC. 964. Any lands which may be discharged from any lien for an assessment for any local improvement or as to which a sale [for non-payment] of *the tax lien thereon for* such assessments authorized to be made by section ten hundred and twenty-seven of this act has been vacated or set aside may be again assessed in the manner provided by law, for such amount as would have been justly chargeable if fraud or irregularity had not been committed; and the amount so assessed shall be a lien on said lands until paid, and shall be collectible in the manner provided by law for the collection of assessments, but all proceedings to make a new assessment shall be at the expense of the city.

SEC. 5. The caption of Title 5 of Chapter XVII. of the Greater New York Charter, as re-enacted by chapter four hundred and sixty-six of the Laws of nineteen hundred and one, is hereby amended so as to read as follows:

Title 5. Sales of *tax liens on* lands for taxes, assessments and water rates.

SEC. 6. Section ten hundred and seventeen of said law is hereby amended so as to read as follows:

WHEN TAXES AND WATER RENTS TO BE LIENS ON LANDS ASSESSED.

SEC. 1017. All taxes and all assessments for local improvements and all water rents, *and the expenses of water meters, with their connections and setting, and water rates and other lawful charges for the supply of water measured by meters,* and the interest and charges thereon, which may, in The City of New York, as by this act constituted, hereafter be laid or may have heretofore been laid, upon any real estate now in said city, shall continue to be, until paid, a lien thereon, and shall be preferred in payment to all other charges. No assessments for any local improvements shall be deemed to be fully confirmed, so as to be due and be a lien upon the property included in the assessment, until ten days after the title thereof, with the date of confirmation shall be entered with the date of such entry, in a record of the titles of assessments confirmed, to be kept in the office of the collector of assessments and arrears.

The words "water rents" whenever they are used in this title shall include, the expenses of meters, with their connections and setting, water rents, water rates and all lawful charges for the supply of water measured by meters.

SEC. 7. Section ten hundred and twenty of the Greater New York Charter is hereby amended so as to read as follows:

RATE.

SEC. 1020. Interest shall hereafter be charged and collected at the rate of seven per centum per annum on all arrears of taxes and assessments returned to the collector of assessments and arrears from the time they become due [until the date of payment, or in case a sale has taken place, as provided in section ten hundred and twenty-seven, until the date of the certificate mentioned in said section] and on [the] *water* rents and [charges for water] *the penalties thereon* from the time the taxes become due, to which they may be added [as required by section ten hundred and twenty-five, until the same date respectively] *until the date of payment, or until such other date when the amount thereof may have been advanced to the city by the purchaser of the tax lien in respect thereof.*

SEC. 8. Section ten hundred and twenty-one of said law is hereby amended so as to read as follows:

APPORTIONMENT OF ASSESSMENT.

SEC. 1021. If a sum of money in gross has been or shall be assessed for local improvements, upon any lands or premises in The City of New York, any person or persons claiming any divided or undivided part thereof may pay such part of the sums of money so assessed, also of the interest and charges due or charged thereon, as the comptroller may deem to be just and equitable. *The board of assessors shall apportion the assessed valuation of such lands or premises when requested by the comptroller so to do, and shall certify such apportionment to him. The determination of the said comptroller shall be based upon such apportionment so certified.* [and] The remainder of the sum of money so assessed, together with the interest and charges, shall be a lien upon the residue of the land and premises only, *and the tax lien upon such* [which] residue may be sold in pursuance of the provisions of this act, to satisfy the residue of such assessment, interest or charges *thereon,* in the same manner as though the residue of said assessment had been imposed upon [the] *such* residue of said land or premises.

SEC. 9. Section ten hundred and twenty-three of said law is hereby amended so as to read as follows:

RECEIVER OF TAXES TO RETURN ARREARS TO THE COLLECTOR.

SEC. 1023. The receiver of taxes shall, on the first day of June, in each year, make a return to the collector of assessments and arrears, of all taxes on real estate and of water [rates and] rents, which have been added thereto, remaining unpaid, and shall notify the comptroller of the aggregate amount of arrears so returned, and balance on his books the accounts of the arrears so returned, by charging the amount thereof to the said collector, and shall thereafter receive no payments on accounts of arrears so returned, but may, nevertheless, certify to the collector of assessments and arrears any errors, which shall, upon such certificate, be corrected by the said collector any time before settlement.

SEC. 10. Section ten hundred and twenty-four of said law is hereby amended so as to read as follows:

WATER RENTS TO BE PROVIDED FOR IN ASSESSMENT-ROLLS.

SEC. 1024. There shall be ruled in the yearly assessment-rolls of each section or ward a column headed " water rents " in which immediately after the confirmation of such assessment-rolls, the collector of assessments and arrears shall cause to be entered opposite the ward, lot, town block and map numbers of the property on which the said arrears may be due, the amounts due for " water rents " *and the expenses of meters, with their connections and setting, water rates and other lawful charges for the supply of water measured by meters,* as transmitted to him by the commissioner of water supply, gas and electricity, in accordance with the law, and the same shall be collected at the same time and in the same manner [with] *as* the taxes to which they shall be added.

SEC. 11. Section ten hundred and twenty-five of said law is hereby amended so as to read as follows:

ARREARS LIKEWISE TO BE PROVIDED FOR.

SEC. 1025. There shall be ruled in the yearly assessment-rolls of the taxes in each section or ward, a column headed "arrears," in which the collector of assessments and arrears shall annually, before any taxes for the year are collected, cause to be entered the word "arrears" [or "sold," according as the fact may be,] opposite to the ward, lot, town block and map numbers on which any arrears of taxes, or of taxes with the water rent added, shall be due, or on which any assessment shall remain unpaid which was due or confirmed one month prior to the first of June, then last past. [or which may have been sold for assessments, taxes or water rents, and yet be redeemable.]

SEC. 12. Section ten hundred and twenty-six of said law is hereby amended so as to read as follows:

BILLS FOR TAXES TO SHOW ARREARS.

SEC. 1026. There shall be ruled a column for "arrears" in every bill rendered for taxes for lots on which said arrears or assessments, or taxes with water rents added, may be due, as aforesaid, [or may have been sold and yet be redeemable,] in which shall be written opposite the entry of the ward, lot, town block and map number of said lot, "arrears" *with the date when such arrears or any part thereof first accrued;* [or "sold," according as the fact may be;] and at the bottom of said bill shall be printed: *"Whenever any tax or assessment shall remain unpaid for three years or any water rent shall remain unpaid for four years the tax lien on the property will be sold to satisfy such arrears of taxes, assessments or water rents, and all taxes, assessments and water rents up to the day of the date of the first advertisement of sale as stated therein"* ["the columns for arrears indicate lots sold for arrears, or to be sold therefor; arrears to be paid and lots redeemed at the office of the collector of assessments and arrears."]

SEC. 13. Section ten hundred and twenty-seven of said law is hereby amended so as to read as follows:

SALES OF [LANDS] *Tax Liens* FOR TAXES AND ASSESSMENTS: PROCEEDINGS.

SEC. 1027. *The right of the city to receive taxes, assessments and water rents and the lien thereof, may be sold by the city, and after such sale, shall be transferred, in the manner provided by this title. The right and lien so sold shall be called "tax lien" and the instrument by which it is assigned shall be called "transfer of tax lien."* Whenever any tax on lands or tenements, or any assessments on lands or tenements for local improvements, shall remain unpaid for the term of three years from the time the same shall have been confirmed, and also whenever any [rents for] water *rents* in said city shall have been due and unpaid for the term of four years from the time the same shall have been due, it shall and may be lawful, for the collector of assessments and arrears, under the direction of the comptroller, to advertise *the tax liens on* the said lands and tenements or any of them for sale, *including in such advertisement the tax lien for all items up to the day of the date of the first advertisement as stated therein* and by such advertisement the owner or owners of such lands and tenements respectively shall be required to pay the amount of such tax, assessment, or water rents, *with the said penalties thereon* so remaining unpaid, together with the interest thereon at the rate of seven per centum per annum to the time of payment, with the charges of such notice and advertisement, to the said collector, and notice shall be given by such advertisement that if default shall be made in such payment *the tax lien on* such lands and tenements will be sold at public auction at a day and place therein to be specified, for the lowest *rate of interest, not exceeding twelve per centum per annum,* [term of years] at which any person or persons shall offer to take the same in consideration of advancing the said tax, assessment [or] *and* water rents *and penalties* as the case may be, [and] the interest thereon as aforesaid to the time of sale, [and] the charges of the above mentioned notices and advertisement and all other costs and charges accrued thereon; and if, notwithstanding such notice, the owner or owners shall refuse or neglect to pay such tax, assessment, [or] water rents *and penalties* with the interests as aforesaid, and the charges attending such notice and advertisement, then it shall and may be lawful for the said collector under the direction of the said comptroller, to cause *such tax lien on* such lands and tenements to be sold at public auction [for a term of years], for the purpose and in the manner expressed in the said advertisement, and such sale shall be made on the day and at the place for that purpose mentioned in the said advertisement, and shall be continued from time to time, if necessary, until all *the tax liens on* the lands and tenements so advertised shall be sold [and the said collector shall give to the purchaser or purchasers of any such lands and tenements a certificate of sale, in writing, describing the lands and tenements so purchased, the term of years for which the same shall have been sold, the sum paid therefor, and the time when the purchaser will be entitled to a lease of the said lands and tenements]. But [no] *the tax lien on* houses or lots, or improved or unimproved lands, in the City of New York, shall *not* be hereafter sold [or leased] at public auction for the non-payment of any tax, assessment, or water rents which may be due thereon, unless notice of such sale shall have been published once in each week successively for three months in the City Record and the corporation newspapers, which advertisement shall contain, appended to said notice, a particular and detailed statement of the property *the tax lien on which is* to be sold. [for taxes, assessments or water rents.] Or the said detailed statement and description, instead of being published in the City Record and the corporation newspapers, shall, at the option of the said comptroller, be printed in a pamphlet, in which case copies of the pamphlet shall be deposited in the office of the said collector, and shall be delivered to any person applying therefor. And the notice provided for in this section to be given of the sale of *tax liens on* houses and lots and improved and unimproved lands shall also state that the detailed statement of the taxes, assessments, or water rents, and [the ownership of] the property [taxes] *taxed,* assessed, [and] *or* on which the water rents are unpaid, is published in the City Record and the corporation newspapers, or in a pamphlet, as the case may be, and that copies of the pamphlet are deposited in the office of said collector, and will be delivered to any person applying for the same. No other notice or demand of the tax, assessment, or water rent shall be required to authorize the sale of *tax liens on* any lands and tenements as hereinbefore provided.

SEC. 14. Section ten hundred and twenty-eight of said law is hereby repealed.

SEC. 15. Section ten hundred and twenty-nine of said law is hereby renumbered so as to be section ten hundred and twenty-eight and is amended so as to read as follows:

POSTPONEMENT OF SALES.

SEC. 1028. It shall be lawful for the comptroller to suspend or postpone any sale or sales of *tax liens on* lands and tenements or any portion thereof which shall have been advertised for sale, to any time not exceeding fifteen months from the day specified in any such advertisement. All sales which shall be postponed or suspended [shall] *may* be made without further advertisement, other than a general notice of such postponement, to be published in the City Record and the corporation newspapers.

SEC. 16. Section ten hundred and thirty of said law is hereby renumbered so as to be section ten hundred and twenty-nine and is amended so as to read as follows:

SALES [FOR TAXES AND ASSESSMENTS] OF TAX LIENS TO BE CONDUCTED BY THE COLLECTOR OF ASSESSMENTS AND ARREARS [: PROVISION FOR REPAYMENT OF PURCHASE MONEY WHEN THE SALE IS VACATED].

SEC. 1029. The collector of assessments and arrears or his assistant shall conduct the sales hereinbefore provided to be made, and no auctioneer other than said collector or his assistant shall be employed to make such sale, and no auctioneers' fees shall be charged thereon. *The comptroller shall require from each purchaser of a tax lien at the time of such sale a deposit on account of the amount of the tax lien purchased by him, and shall prescribe a time not later than thirty days from the date of sale, when the balance shall be paid to the collector of assessments and arrears, at his office. Transfers of tax lien* [certificates of sale] shall be made and delivered to the purchaser without charge upon payment of the amounts therein shown to be due. [And all certificates of sale not paid for within thirty days following the date of sale, may be canceled by the collector of assessments and arrears and the sales relating thereto declared void. In case any sale shall be vacated or canceled, the purchaser, his legal representative or assign, shall be repaid the amount paid by him at such sale, with interest thereon from the time of such payment.] *In case any purchaser shall not complete his purchase in accordance with the terms prescribed as herein provided, then the amount deposited by him at the time of the sale shall be forfeited to the city, and the entire tax lien upon the lands affected by such purchase shall be sold again. Such resale shall be held at such time as the comptroller may direct and shall be advertised in the City Record and the corporation newspapers, in such manner and for such time, not less than two weeks, as the comptroller may direct. All deposits forfeited as aforesaid shall be paid into the General Fund of the City of New York.*

SEC. 17. Sections ten hundred and thirty-one to ten hundred and forty-nine, both inclusive, of said law are hereby repealed.

SEC. 18. The said law is hereby amended by adding thereto a new section, to be section ten hundred and thirty, and to read as follows:

TRANSFERS OF TAX LIENS.

SEC. 1030. A transfer of tax lien shall operate to transfer and assign the tax lien upon the lands or tenements described therein for the taxes, assessments and water rents, and penalties, the interest thereon, and the charges of the notices and advertisement given pursuant to section ten hundred and twenty-seven of this act, and all other costs and charges, so advertised for sale, free of all taxes, assessments and water rents, constituting such tax lien, which were mentioned in such advertisement of sale, but subject to the lien for and right of the city to collect and receive all taxes, assessments and water rents which accrued or which became a lien on and after the day of the date of the first advertisement of such sale as stated therein. A transfer of tax lien shall contain a transfer and assignment by the city of the tax lien sold to the purchaser, the date of the sale, the aggregate amount of the tax lien so transferred, and the items of taxes, assessments, water rents, penalties, and interest composing the tax lien, the annual rate of interest which the purchaser has bid and will be entitled to receive, the date when the amount of the tax lien will be due, and a description of the real property affected by the tax lien, which description shall include the name of the borough in which the property lies and shall refer for certainty to the designation of said lot on the tax map, by its lot number and the number of the block, ward or section in which it is contained, and such other identifying description as the collector of assessments and arrears may deem proper to add. Each transfer of tax lien shall be subscribed by or in behalf of the collector of assessments and arrears, making the sale or a successor in office of such collector, and shall be acknowledged by the officer subscribing the same in the manner in which a deed is required to be acknowledged to be recorded in the county in which the real property affected is situated.

SEC. 19. The said law is hereby amended by adding thereto a new section to be section ten hundred and thirty-one and to read as follows:

RECORD OF TRANSFERS OF TAX LIENS.

SEC. 1031. The collector of assessments and arrears shall keep in his office a public record of sales of tax liens, and a copy of each transfer of tax lien issued by him. A transfer of tax lien and any assignment thereof, duly acknowledged, shall be deemed conveyances under Article VIII. of the Real Property Law, and may be recorded in the office of the recording officer of any county in which the real property which it affects is situated. Transfers of tax lien and all assignments thereof shall be recorded by recording officers in the same manner as mortgages and assignments thereof, but without payment of tax under Article XIV. of the Tax Law. The record in the office of the collector of assessments and arrears of sales of tax liens, of a transfer of tax lien, and of a copy of a transfer tax lien; a record of a transfer tax lien in the office of a recording officer, and of an assignment of tax lien, duly acknowledged, in the office of a recording officer, shall each be evidence in any court in the state without further proof. A transcript of any record enumerated in this section, duly certified, shall be evidence in any court in the state with like effect as the original instrument of record. Neither the tax lien nor the rights transferred by a transfer tax lien shall be impaired by failure to record the transfer of tax lien in the office of a recording officer. Unless a contrary intent appears, a tax lien shall be presumed to be merged with the title of the owner in fee simple of the lands or tenements described therein whenever it shall appear from recorded instruments that the tax lien has been transferred or assigned to the owner of such lands or tenements, notwithstanding other intervening estates or liens.

SEC. 20. The said law is hereby amended by adding thereto a new section, to be section ten hundred and thirty-two, and to read as follows:

Rights of Purchaser of Tax Lien.

Sec. 1032. The aggregate amount of each tax lien transferred pursuant to this title, shall be due three years from the date of the sale. Until such aggregate amount is fully paid and discharged, the holder of the transfer of tax lien shall be entitled to receive interest on such aggregate amount from the day of sale, semi-annually on the first day of January and July, at the rate which the purchaser shall have bid. At the option of the holder of any transfer of tax lien the aggregate amount thereof shall become due and payable after default in the payment of interest for thirty days or after default for six months after the delivery of transfer tax lien in the payment of any taxes, assessments or water rents, which become a lien on and after the day of the date of the first advertisement of the sale as stated therein, of the tax lien transferred by such transfer of tax lien. Any person having a legal or beneficial interest in property affected by a transfer of tax lien may satisfy the same before maturity upon giving thirty days' notice in writing to the holder thereof, of the day on which payment will be made and upon payment of the principal with interest at the rate bid to a time three months after the day so fixed for payment. If notice of intention to make payment be given as herein provided, and such payment be not made, then the whole amount of any tax lien concerning which such notice shall have been given shall become due and payable at the option of the holder thereof. Or any such person may pay to the collector of assessments and arrears such principal with interest at the rate bid up to a day six months after such payment. In case such payment be made to the collector of assessments and arrears he shall receive the same for the benefit of the holder of the tax lien thus discharged, and shall give notice thereof to the purchaser or the personal representative or assignee of the purchaser, by mail addressed to such address as may have been furnished to the collector of assessments and arrears. Upon receiving surrender of such transfer tax lien the collector of assessments and arrears shall pay to the person entitled thereto the amount thus deposited.

Sec. 21. The said law is hereby amended by adding thereto a new section, to be section ten hundred and thirty-three, and to read as follows:

Discharge of Tax Lien.

Sec. 1033. A tax lien sold pursuant to the provisions of this title must be discharged upon the record thereof by the collector of assessments and arrears when payment is made to him of the principal and interest as provided in the last preceding section, and also when the transfer of tax lien is surrendered to him for cancellation and there is presented to him a certificate executed by the purchaser, or the personal representative or assignee of the purchaser, acknowledged so as to be entitled to be recorded in the county in which the real property affected by such tax lien is situated, certifying that the tax lien has been paid or has been otherwise satisfied and discharged. The transfer of tax lien thus surrendered and such certificate of discharge must be filed by the collector of assessments and arrears and he must note upon the margin of the record of such sale, upon such transfer of tax lien and upon the copy of the transfer of tax lien kept in his office a minute of such discharge and the date of filing thereof. If the transfer of tax lien shall have been lost or destroyed or mutilated, application for an order dispensing with the production of the transfer of tax lien may be made in the same manner as is provided in section two hundred and seventy-a of the Real Property Law, the provisions of which so far as the same may be, are hereby made applicable to discharge of tax liens. The collector of assessments and arrears shall upon demand issue his certificate showing the discharge of any tax lien which may have been duly discharged as provided in this section, and such certificate may be filed in any office where the transfer of tax lien is recorded, and any recording officer with whom such a certificate is filed, shall record the same, and upon the margin of the record of such transfer of tax lien in his office shall note a statement that the same has been discharged with a reference to the record of such certificate in his office.

Sec. 22. The said law is hereby amended by adding thereto a new section, to be section ten hundred and thirty-four, and to read as follows:

Exemption from Taxation.

Sec. 1034. Tax liens and transfers of tax liens shall be exempt from taxation by the state or any local subdivisions thereof, except from the taxes imposed by article ten of the tax law. The real property affected by any tax lien shall not be exempt from taxation by reason of this section.

SEC. 23. The said law is hereby amended by adding thereto a new section, to be section ten hundred and thirty-five, and to read as follows:

FORECLOSURE OF TAX LIEN.

SEC. 1035. If the amount of any tax lien which shall have been transferred by a transfer of tax lien shall not be paid when under its terms and the provisions of this title such amount shall be due, the holder of such tax lien may maintain an action in the Supreme Court to foreclose such tax lien. In an action to foreclose a tax lien any person shall be a proper party of whom the plaintiff alleges that such person has or may have or that the plaintiff has reason to believe that such person has or may have, an interest in or claim upon the real property affected by the tax lien. Except as otherwise provided in this title an action to foreclose a tax lien shall be regulated by the provisions of the Code of Civil Procedure and by all other provisions of law, and rules of practice applicable to actions to foreclose mortgages on real property. The People of the State of New York may be made party to an action to foreclose a tax lien in the same manner as a natural person.

SEC. 24. The said law is hereby amended by adding thereto a new section, to be section ten hundred and thirty-six, and to read as follows:

PLEADING TRANSFER OF TAX LIEN.

SEC. 1036. Whenever a cause of action, defense or counterclaim, is for the foreclosure of a tax lien, or is in any manner founded upon a tax lien or a transfer of tax lien, if in any pleading or petition, there be set forth a copy of a transfer of tax lien, together with a statement of the time and place of the recording thereof in the office of the collector of assessments and arrears or in any other public office, it shall not be necessary to plead or prove any act, proceeding, notice or action preceding the issue of such transfer of tax sale, nor to establish the validity of the tax lien transferred by such transfer of tax lien. If a party or person in interest in any such action or proceeding claims that a tax lien is irregular or invalid, or that there is any defect therein or that a transfer of tax is irregular, invalid or defective, such invalidity, irregularity or defect must be specifically pleaded or set forth, and must be established affirmatively by the party or person pleading or setting forth the same.

SEC. 25. The said law is hereby amended by adding thereto a new section, to be section ten hundred and thirty-seven, and to read as follows:

JUDGMENT UPON TAX LIEN.

SEC. 1037. In every action for the foreclosure of a tax lien, and in every action or proceeding in which a cause of action, defense or counterclaim is in any manner founded upon a tax lien or a transfer of tax lien, such transfer of tax lien and the tax lien which it transfers shall be presumed to be regular and valid and effectual to transfer to the purchaser named therein a valid and enforcible tax lien. Unless in such an action or proceeding such tax lien or transfer of tax lien be found to be invalid it shall be lawful in any interlocutory or final judgment, or any final order entered therein, to adjudge that a tax lien transferred by a transfer of tax lien pleaded or set forth as provided in section ten hundred and thirty-six, or a tax lien established or proved in any other manner to the satisfaction of the court, is a valid lien upon all or part of the real property which it purports to affect, and that the transfer of tax lien transferring the same is effectual to transfer such tax lien to the purchaser named therein.

SEC. 26. The said law is hereby amended by adding thereto a new section, to be section ten hundred and thirty-eight, and to read as follows:

JUDGMENT OF FORECLOSURE OF TAX LIEN.

SEC. 1038. In an action to foreclose a tax lien, unless the defendants obtain judgment, the plaintiff shall be entitled to a judgment establishing the validity of the tax lien so far as the same shall not be adjudged invalid and of the transfer of tax lien, and directing the sale of the real property affected thereby, or such part thereof as shall be sufficient to discharge the tax lien, or such items thereof as shall not be adjudged invalid, and all other accrued taxes, assessments and water rents affecting the real property, together with the expenses of the sale, and the costs of the action.

SEC. 27. The said law is hereby amended by adding thereto a new section, to be section ten hundred and thirty-nine, and to read as follows:

Effect of Judgment Foreclosing Tax Lien.

Sec. 1039. Every final judgment in an action to foreclose a tax lien shall be binding upon, and every conveyance upon a sale pursuant thereto, shall transfer to and vest in the purchaser all the right, title, interest and estate in and claim upon the real property affected by such judgment, of, the plaintiff, each defendant, whether individual or trustee, upon whom the summons is served, each person claiming from, through or under such a defendant by title accruing after the filing of notice of pendency of the action or after the entry of judgment and filing of the judgment roll in the proper county clerk's office, and each person not in being when the judgment is rendered, who afterwards may become entitled to a beneficial interest attaching to, or an estate or interest in such real property or any portion thereof, provided that the person first entitled to such beneficial interest, estate or interest is a party to such action or bound by such judgment. So much of section four hundred and forty-five of the Code of Civil Procedure as requires the court to allow a defendant to defend an action after final judgment shall not apply to an action to foreclose a tax lien. Delivery of the possession of real property affected by a judgment to foreclose a tax lien may be compelled in the manner prescribed in section sixteen hundred and seventy-five of the Code of Civil Procedure.

Sec. 28. The said law is hereby amended by adding thereto a new section, to be section ten hundred and forty, and to read as follows:

Surplus.

Sec. 1040. Any surplus of the proceeds of the sale, after paying the expenses of the sale, and all taxes, assessments and water rents which accrued or became a lien on and after the day of the date of the first advertisement of the sale as stated therein, under which the foreclosed transfer of tax lien was issued, and satisfying the amount of the tax lien and interest and the costs of the action, must be paid into court, for the use of the person or persons entitled thereto. If any part of the surplus remains in court for the period of three months, and no application has been made therefor, the court must, and, if an application therefor is pending, the court may direct such surplus to be invested at interest, for the benefit of the person or persons entitled thereto, to be paid upon the direction of the court.

SEC. 29. The said law is hereby amended by adding thereto a new section, to be section ten hundred and forty-one, and to read as follows:

FORECLOSED TAX LIEN NOT ARREARS.

SEC. 1041. Any party to an action to foreclose a tax lien or any purchaser or any party in interest may give notice of such foreclosure to the collector of assessments and arrears, and after such notice the items which constituted the tax lien thus foreclosed shall not be entered by the collector of assessments and arrears in any yearly assessment roll, so long as the judgment of foreclosure of such lien remains in force.

SEC. 30. The said law is hereby amended by adding thereto a new section, to be section ten hundred and forty-two, and to read as follows:

PROCEDURE WHEN NO BID FOR A TAX LIEN IS RECEIVED.

SEC. 1042. If no bid be received for a tax lien on any parcel of property at a duly advertised sale and it shall appear to the comptroller that the taxes, assessments, water rents, penalties and accrued interest amount to so large a proportion of the value of the property that the security is insufficient to attract bidders, then and in that event the comptroller and the corporation counsel shall investigate the facts and may fix a lesser amount for which in their judgment a tax lien bearing twelve per centum interest can be sold. A certificate in writing, signed by them, shall be filed with the collector of assessments and arrears, setting forth the amount so determined by them, together with a brief statement of the reasons for such reduction, which certificate shall include the total amount of the taxes, assessments, water rents, penalties and accrued interest, the assessed value of such parcel of real estate, and the value of the land as the same appears on the last preceding assessment roll. Thereafter such reduced amount shall constitute the tax lien upon said real property for the items therein enumerated, which reduced amount shall bear interest at the rate of seven per cent. per annum from the date of such certificate until fully paid, or until the tax lien thus fixed, together with the lien for any other taxes, assessments, water rents, and penalties and interest becoming liens thereafter shall be sold. The collector of assessments and arrears shall forthwith advertise the tax lien for such reduced amount for sale to the highest bidder in the manner provided for the advertisement for the sale of ordinary tax liens. Such tax lien shall bear interest at twelve per centum and shall be sold to the person bidding the highest amount of money in excess of the reduced amount so fixed by the comptroller and corporation counsel, provided that if the bidding reaches the original amount of the tax lien on the real property affected, the sale shall proceed in the manner provided in section ten hundred and twenty-nine. If no bid shall be received at such sale, the comptroller and corporation counsel shall reconsider their determination and may file a new certificate in the manner hereinbefore provided, and the collector of assessments and arrears shall proceed again as hereinbefore directed. Such procedure shall be repeated until a tax lien for such taxes, assessments, water rents and accrued interest shall be sold.

SEC. 31. The said law is hereby amended by adding thereto a new section, to be section ten hundred and forty-three, and to read as follows:

REIMBURSEMENT FOR DEFECTIVE TAX LIENS OR TRANSFERS OF TAX LIENS.

SEC. 1043. If a transfer of tax lien be vacated or be set aside or canceled, or if it be adjudged in any action that a transfer of tax lien is invalid or defective, or not sufficient to transfer a tax lien to the purchaser thereof, or if in any action to foreclose a tax lien, it be adjudged that the entire tax lien is void and not a valid lien on the premises which it purports to affect, and that the complaint be dismissed, the purchaser may surrender such transfer of tax lien to the collector of assessments and arrears and thereupon shall be repaid by the city the amount paid for such transfer of tax lien, with interest from the time of such payment at the rate set forth in the transfer of tax lien, and the city shall pay the taxed costs and disbursements of any action or proceeding in which such adjudication is made.

SEC. 32. The said law is hereby amended by adding thereto a new section, to be section ten hundred and forty-four, and to read as follows:

REIMBURSEMENT WHEN PART OF TAX LIEN IS DEFECTIVE.

SEC. 1044. If, in any action to foreclose a tax lien, it shall be adjudged that some, but not all of the items constituting such tax lien are void and not a valid lien on the premises covered by such tax lien, or if in any action or proceeding it be adjudged that a transfer of tax lien is invalid or defective, as to some though not as to all of the items transferred, the holder of the transfer of tax lien, by instrument in writing duly acknowledged, shall retransfer to the city the items thus affected, and shall be repaid by the city such portion of the amount paid for such transfer of tax lien as may be applicable to the items thus affected, with interest from the time of such payment at the rate set forth in the transfer of tax lien, and the city shall pay the taxed costs and disbursements of any action or proceeding, other than an action to foreclose the tax lien, in which such adjudication is made.

SEC. 33. The said law is hereby amended by adding thereto a new section, to be section ten hundred and forty-five, and to read as follows:

OWNERS MAY QUESTION TRANSFERS OF TAX LIENS.

SEC. 1045. Any person interested in or holding a lien upon any real property affected by any unpaid tax lien or transfer of tax lien, may file a written notice with the collector of assessments and arrears claiming that a transfer of tax lien is invalid or defective or that a tax lien which has been transferred pursuant to this title or which is advertised to be transferred is invalid, defective, void or ineffectual, or should be vacated or set aside. The collector of assessments and arrears shall transmit all such notices to the corporation counsel, who shall examine into the facts and proceedings resulting in the tax lien or transfer of a tax lien mentioned in such notice; before a determination is had the corporation counsel shall serve a copy of such notice upon the holder of the transfer of tax lien which is thus questioned or which transfers the items thus questioned and shall give such holder an opportunity to be heard. The corporation counsel shall certify in writing his opinion upon the matters and questions raised by such notice, and if he concludes that a defense in an action to foreclose the tax lien would succeed in whole or in part he shall so certify, and shall recommend what action shall be taken by the city concerning the same. If the corporation counsel concludes that such defense would succeed in whole or in part and recommends repayment by the city of the amount paid for a transfer of tax lien which would be applicable to any item, he shall state the reasons for such recommendation, and if it be approved by the mayor and comptroller the city shall require the surrender of the transfer of tax lien or the retransfer to it of the item or items of tax lien which are found to be void or defective, and shall make repayment therefor in the same manner as if such transfer of tax lien, tax lien or items had been adjudicated in the manner provided in sections ten hundred and forty-three and ten hundred and forty-four. Neither the provisions of this section nor any act or proceeding thereunder shall impair or in any other manner affect the rights or remedies of any person interested in, or holding any lien upon, real property to question the validity of any tax, assessment, water rents or tax lien, or any part or item of any tax lien.

SEC. 34. The said law is hereby amended by adding thereto a new section, to be section ten hundred and forty-six, and to read as follows:

CORPORATION COUNSEL TO PROTECT INTEREST OF CITY.

SEC. 1046. No claim shall be made against the city under sections ten hundred and forty-three, ten hundred and forty-four or ten hundred and forty-five by the holder of any tax lien, unless action to foreclose the tax lien or transfer of tax lien upon which such claim is founded be commenced within five years from the time of the sale resulting in such transfer of tax lien. Nor shall any claim be made against the city under sections ten hundred and forty-three or ten hundred and forty-four, unless within ten days after the commencement of any action or proceeding to vacate, set aside or cancel a transfer of tax lien, or a tax lien or an item mentioned in a transfer of tax lien, or unless within ten days after the service of any pleading or other paper in an action or proceeding in which any tarnsfer of tax lien, or item mentioned in a transfer of tax lien, is brought into question, sought to be set aside, vacated, or canceled, or which sets forth or pleads any defense to an action to foreclose a tax lien, a notice in writing be served upon the corporation counsel setting forth the question or objection raised to the best knowledge of the holder of the transfer of tax lien, or his attorney at law, and demanding that the city take up the prosecution or defense of the action or proceeding. All proceedings in such action or proceeding shall be stayed for thirty days or such shorter time as the corporation counsel shall stipulate in writing. It shall be the duty of the corporation counsel to examine the questions raised, and, in order to protect the interests of the city, he shall have the right to be substituted for the attorney of record of the holder of the transfer tax lien, or to appear as attorney of record for the holder of any such transfer of tax lien, to conduct or defend any such action or proceeding in the name of the holder of the transfer of tax lien, and to bring any other action or proceeding for, on behalf of and in the name of the holder of such transfer of tax lien as he may deem advisable, to take appeals, and to argue appeals taken by the adverse party, as he may deem advisable. It shall be the duty of the corporation counsel to protect the interest of the city in all matters, actions and proceedings relating to tax liens and transfers of tax liens; to intervene on behalf of the city or of the holder of a transfer of tax lien in, or to make the city a party to any action in which he believes it to be to the interest of the city so to do, by reason of any matter arising under or relating to any tax lien or transfer of tax lien, or advertisement of sale of tax liens. In any action or proceeding in which the corporation counsel pursuant to this section shall be substituted, or shall appear, it shall be without expense to the holder of the transfer of tax lien, and all costs recovered on behalf of such holder of a transfer of tax lien in any action or proceeding conducted or defended by the corporation counsel shall belong to the city and shall be collected, applied and disposed of in the same manner as are other costs recovered by the city.

SEC. 35. The said law is hereby amended by adding thereto a new section, to be section ten hundred and forty-seven, and to read as follows:

DEFECTIVE OR INVALID TRANSFER OF TAX LIEN; PROCEEDING ANEW.

SEC. 1047. If a transfer of tax lien be vacated or be set aside or canceled or it be adjudged that a transfer of tax lien is invalid or defective, or insufficient to transfer a tax lien to the purchaser thereof, or if in any action to foreclose a tax lien, it be adjudged that a tax lien is not a valid lien on the premises which it purports to affect, because of some irregularity in the proceedings had, and if, in pursuance of any such adjudication the purchaser of said transfer of tax lien shall have surrendered such transfer of tax lien to the collector of assessments and arrears and shall have been repaid by the city, the amount paid for such transfer of tax lien, with interest and costs and disbursements of the said action or proceeding in which such adjudication was made, then and in that event, the tax lien which was purported to be transferred and assigned in such transfer of tax lien shall remain as a valid lien upon the premises which it affects, except to such extent as it may have been adjudged irregular or invalid, and the collector of assessments and arrears shall proceed to sell anew, as provided in section ten hundred and twenty-seven of this act, so much of the said tax lien as is not invalid as if no prior sale purporting to transfer the said tax lien had taken place.

SEC. 36. Section ten hundred and fifty of said law is hereby renumbered so as to be section ten hundred and forty-eight and amended so as to read as follows:

LOST [CERTIFICATE] *Transfer of Tax Lien* DELIVERY OF [LEASE] *Duplicate* IN CASE OF.

SEC. 1048. Whenever any [certificate] *transfer of tax lien* given by the collector of assessments and arrears, as in this title provided, [of land sold] shall be lost, the [said] comptroller may receive evidence of such loss, and on satisfactory proof of the fact may *direct the collector of assessments and arrears to* execute and deliver a [lease] *duplicate* to such person or persons who shall appear entitled thereto [of the lands and tenements described in the certificate], and may also, in his discretion, require a bond of indemnity to The City of New York. [Each certificate shall be registered in the record of sales to be kept in the bureau of said collector of assessments and arrears, and no transfer of such certificate shall be valid until registered in said book.]

SEC. 37. Section ten hundred and fifty-one of said law is hereby renumbered so as to be section ten hundred and forty-nine, and amended so as to read as follows:

BILLS OF ARREARS OF TAXES AND ASSESSMENTS TO BE FURNISHED WHEN REQUESTED.

SEC. 1049. The collector of assessments and arrears, upon the requisition of any person, shall furnish a bill of all arrears of taxes, and of taxes with the "water rents" added on any lot or lots due prior to the first of June, then last past, and of assessments which are due and payable [including the amount necessary to redeem it or them, if it or they have been sold for any arrears of assessments, taxes or water rents and be yet redeemable]; and upon the payment of the said bill (which shall be called a "bill of arrears and assessments, taxes and water rents,") [and for redemption] his receipt thereon, countersigned by the comptroller, shall be conclusive evidence of such payment. The comptroller shall cause to be kept a duplicate account of amounts, so collected, and the certificate of the collector of assessments and arrears, countersigned by the comptroller, that there are no [such] *tax* liens on said lot or lots, shall forever free the said lot or lots from all liens of taxes, or for taxes with water rates added, or for rents of water added to the taxes prior to the first of June then last past, and for all assessments due and payable prior to the date of the said receipt or certificate, *but not from the lien of any tax lien duly sold* [and from all liens in consequence of sales for assessments, taxes, or water rents, or for all of them, when the time allowed by law for redemption had not expired at the date or time of said payment or certificate.]

SEC. 38. Section ten hundred and fifty-two of said law is hereby renumbered so as to be section ten hundred and fifty.

SEC. 39. Section ten hundred and fifty-three of said law is hereby repealed.

SEC. 40. Section ten hundred and fifty-four of said law is hereby renumbered so as to be section ten hundred and fifty-one.

SEC. 41. This act shall not affect or impair any act done or right accruing, accrued or acquired, nor any penalty or forfeiture incurred prior to the time when this act takes effect, by virtue of any section of the Greater New York Charter repealed, amended or modified by this act; but such right, penalty, or forfeiture, may be asserted, enforced, prosecuted or inflicted as fully and to the same extent as if this act had not been passed or said sections had not been amended, repealed or modified; no tax lease heretofore issued nor any tax sale heretofore made shall be affected by this act, but the rights of all persons, with respect thereto, shall be the same as if this act had not been passed, and all actions, suits, proceedings or prosecutions under the sections of Title 5 of Chapter XVII. of the Greater New York Charter hereby amended, repealed or modified and pending when this act takes effect may be prosecuted and defended to final effect in the same manner as they might prior to the time when this act takes effect.

SEC. 42. This act shall take effect January first, 1909.

TAX LIENS MADE LEGAL INVESTMENTS FOR SAVINGS BANKS.

In order that there may be as wide a market as possible for the sale of tax liens, it is proposed that they shall be a legal investment for savings banks, the following bill is, therefore, proposed to accomplish this object:

AN ACT to amend the Banking Law by providing that tax liens of The City of New York shall be lawful investments for savings banks.

The People of the State of New York, represented in Senate and Assembly, do enact as follows:

SEC. 1. Subdivision four of section one hundred sixteen of chapter six hundred eighty-nine of the Laws of eighteen hundred and ninety-two, being chapter thirty-seven of the General Laws, as amended by chapter three hundred twenty-eight of the Laws of nineteen hundred and three, is hereby amended so as to read as follows:

4. *In transfers of tax liens of the City of New York where the amount of tax liens does not exceed half the assessed value of the real property encumbered thereby,* in the stocks or bonds of any city, county, town or village, school district bonds and union free school district bonds issued for school purposes, or in the interest bearing obligations of any city, county, town or village of this State, issued pursuant to the authority of any law of the state, for the payment of which the faith and credit of the municipality issuing them are pledged.

SEC. 2. This act shall take effect the first day of January, nineteen hundred and nine.

INDEX.

www.ingramcontent.com/pod-product-compliance
Lightning Source LLC
LaVergne TN
LVHW021401110826
845150LV00007B/1735

* 9 7 8 1 4 2 5 5 1 3 5 9 7 *